Simplifying Relationships

A concise guide to dealing with other people, living your best life and connecting in disconnected times.

Jody Andrews

Dedicated to my clients and students
from whom I have learned much.
And to George and Becky
who made it all work.

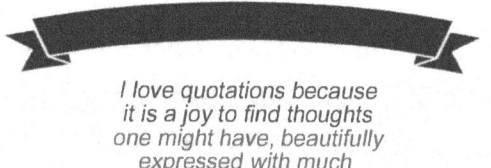

I love quotations because it is a joy to find thoughts one might have, beautifully expressed with much authority by someone recognized wiser than oneself. –Marlene Dietrich

Table of Contents

Introduction

*Our greatest joy and our greatest pain comes in our
relationships with others.*
−Stephen R. Covey

The trouble with relationships is other people. We have friends and neighbors, partners and lovers. We live in communities. We come from families, and we earn our living working with or for other people. This book utilizes tools to help you determine if a relationship is healthy and offer solutions for change if necessary. This book will also help you understand what might be keeping you stuck in a difficult situation and learn what to expect when dealing with transitions and loss. And it will also help you learn to live your best life and to connect more fully with others. Each chapter incorporates quotes and graphics to make you think, feel and even smile. Terms or concepts to explore outside of the scope of this book are expressed in italics. It is a book to come back to again and again to help you make informed decisions about life and relationships. My hope is you share this book and your own stories with others to create a sense of gen-uine community and connection.

CHAPTER 1

The Essentials

Life is really simple, but we insist on

making it complicated.

–Confucius

Essentials

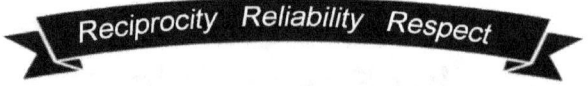

Reciprocity   Reliability   Respect

Living in a world that includes other people is challenging. Because we are all complex human beings, it is impossible to define a set protocol, formula or blueprint to work from. For most relationships, you can utilize these three essential elements: reciprocity of effort, reliability of commitment and respect for values as a baseline for determining success. These are the basic behaviors - essentially just plain good manners, for any relationship to feel healthy, meaningful and emotionally fulfilling. While it will not solve every dilemma in dealing with others, it is a good place to start.

Reciprocity

There is one word which may serve as a rule of practice for all

one's life-reciprocity

−Confucius

Reciprocity of effort means that equivalent energy is being put forth to initiate and maintain a relationship. This does not mean the receiving party must reciprocate immediately or in kind - just that overall, over time, a healthy relationship is based on giving and receiving and the relationship is balanced. An unevenness in reciprocity indicates there is an imbalance of power. If we find ourselves in a situation with repeated unreciprocated patterns of interacting, we can become resentful, hurt, angry and depressed. This can lead to underlying physical and mental health issues and/or the failure of the relationship. Reciprocity matters!

Reliability

Trust should be guarded to the end: without trust we cannot stand.

−Confucius

Reliability of commitment begs the questions: Can I trust you? Can I count on you? Do you do what you say you will do and when you say you will do it? − Do you walk the walk, talk the talk, do as you say and say as you do? You get the idea. Without reliability, trust and predictability, our world lacks certainty. The ground feels shaky. We can become anxious. Reliability, trust and predictability appeal to our basic sense of safety and security. If you find yourself in a situation that feels uncertain, inconsistent and precarious, it is time to step back and reevaluate. Reliability matters!

Respect

Respect yourself and others will respect you.

−Confucius

Respect means non-violation. It means being seen and feeling heard. It means you are aware of the differences and choose to "live and let live" as best you can. Respect does not mean agreement or compliance. It does not mean being liked or liking the other. It means being respected for who you are. This includes respect for who you love, what you believe. what you do, your boundaries, your time. Will you treat me with dignity? Respect matters!

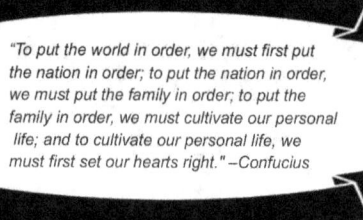

"To put the world in order, we must first put the nation in order; to put the nation in order, we must put the family in order; to put the family in order, we must cultivate our personal life; and to cultivate our personal life, we must first set our hearts right." –Confucius

CHAPTER 2

The Toolbox

It's best to have your tools with you. If you don't, you're

apt to find something you didn't expect and get

discouraged.

−Stephen King

The Toolbox

Checklists, Flags, Circles, Reflections

Years ago, a client left me a very special gift. A small tin toy tool-box with miniature tools glued to the outside. Inside were index cards written with many of the therapeutic tools and interventions we had shared. It is one of the inspirations for this book - the toolbox. We need to take in information repeatedly and in a variety of ways before we truly learn and integrate it into our brain. For something to become a habitual way of thinking takes weeks or even months. Most of us are visual learners and many of us learn best by experiencing or "doing". To that end we will be working with different methods of assessing relationships and doing it repeatedly. If one gets in the habit of thinking about relationships based on the three essentials while using these tools, it may help avoid unforeseen pitfalls.

Checklists

I watch a lot of astronaut movies...Mostly Star Wars. And even

Han and Chewie use a checklist.

–Jon Stewart

Checklists "keep us in check". (Duh). Sometimes our brain needs a guide to keep us from going off the rails. Use a list, just as you would when starting any project or even going to the grocery store. The idea is getting us to think, organize and plan. The physical act of finding a pen or pencil and going over the list is another way of maintaining a sense of control over a questionable situation.

Circles

Draw a circle around yourself, - invite people in or keep them out.

−Rachel Wolchin

Visualizing concentric circles is a useful tool for defining or accepting the limits of relationships. You might think of it as your "inner" "middle" and "outer" circle of people in your life. Outer circles are casual acquaintances, middle for those with more interaction, and inner for those close to you. I view the outer ring as representing reciprocity, the middle ring reliability, and the inside as respect. Whichever way works best for you. The goal is for this way of thinking to become a habit. When all three of the essentials are present: reciprocity, reliability, and respect, I visualize a three-circle relationship with me inside − protected and insulated. You may choose to assign it an "inner circle" relationship. Thinking in relationship circles makes it easier to accept the limitations of others.

Flags

The red flags are usually there, you just have to keep your eyes
open wider than your heart.

–April Mae Monterrosa

A colorful and experiential way to assess the health of a relationship is to create your own mini flag display. It is especially handy when dating. Make a handful of each: green, yellow and red flags from sticky notes and stir sticks. Plant in a small flowerpot filled with beans or pebbles. While you are evaluating a relationship, pay close attention to what is said and done. Assess your observations and interaction(s) based on the three essentials: reciprocity, reliability and respect. Plant green flags realistically with your eyes wide open. Yellow flags are for those areas of uncertainty - proceed with caution. Red flags are for those behaviors that give you pause and serious concern. Trust your intuition - it may save future frustration and heartache.

Self Reflection

All relationship is a reflection of your relationship with yourself.

–Deepak Chopra

Self reflection takes courage. It's tough, and it's important. It keeps us from being a victim. We may discover we have more power and choice in determining the direction of a particular relationship than we thought. We realize we may not want to put in the effort to make it reciprocal. Or maybe we have been less than reliable in our commitments. We may have to admit that we are not tolerant and respectful of others as we thought. Ask the tough questions: In this relationship, am I reciprocal? Am I reliable? Am I respectful? Awareness of our desires and limitations makes it easier to choose a direction or solution.

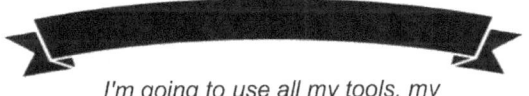

*I'm going to use all my tools, my
God-given ability, and make the
best life I can with it.*
–LeBron James

CHAPTER 3

Solutions

For every complex problem, there's a solution that is

simple, neat, and wrong.

–H.L. Mencken

Solutions

Do Nothing   Communicate   Leave

When it is time to address issues in your relationships your choices come down to three basic options: *do nothing, communicate* or *leave*. Within each are infinite variations. Before you explore your options decide: Am I willing to risk losing? We have no power unless we are ready to walk away. Also ask yourself: Is it more important that I be *liked* or that I be *respected* in this situation? You must decide which to lead with. Choose your left foot or right foot - you cannot do both or you'd be hopping like a bunny. When we want to be liked we tend to over-accommodate, sometimes called *toxic niceness*. While it may mean a short-term bump in popularity, in the long run it can invite contempt. When we want to be respected, we tend to set firm boundaries and say no when we mean no. Initially, it might feel like we are creating conflict, or being seen as cold and intimidating, but generally, respect leads to healthier outcomes.

Do Nothing

Don't underestimate the value of Doing Nothing, of just going along,
listening to all the things you can't hear, and not bothering.

–AA Milne

Doing nothing by choice can be a very potent option. There is power in not responding. Think of it as being a Zen Master. Wait and see. Your perspective may change. The other party may change their perception. The situation may resolve itself. Do not confuse deliberately doing nothing with the silent treatment. This is passive-aggressive. Use your down time constructively: reframe your circumstances, savor the small things that give you pleasure, practice gratitude. Sit still. Breathe. It defies expectations and is more dignified than "losing it" in the more typical reaction.

Communicate

Etiquette is really about being respectful and honest with individuals and speaking your truth.

−Elaine Swann

Texting has become our "go to" for more informal means of communication. It is easy, and if it is short (as it should be) takes less than a minute. A reply takes ten seconds. Less if you just do an emoji. An unanswered text can create anxiety. A Google research study found that 20 minutes was the magic number for a desired response. This is not always practical. While the exact amount of time is debatable among etiquette experts, somewhere between 24 and 48 hours seems an acceptable range. Then you may send a second quick reminder text. Still no response? Etiquette expert Diane Gottsman weighs in with: "If someone 'ghosts' you, take the hint and walk away. You do not deserve to be treated disrespectfully. Don't continue to reach out to someone who will not respond back and think carefully about the excuses they give once they pop back in your life several months later."

Leave

It is so hard to leave—until you leave. And then it is the easiest
goddamned thing in the world.

—John Green

Sometimes you just need to invoke the baseball rule - three
strikes and you are *out*. When you are ready you will know.
There is strength in leaving. Get started and keep going. Leave
with your dignity intact. With most relationship endings there is
a mix of emotion. Feelings of anger, guilt, fear, depression, anxiety and relief. Going through the *process of grief* is normal and
necessary. You may be grieving the loss of illusion, which is often a greater loss than the loss of reality. It may be the death of
a future full of hopes, dreams, security, comfort, companionship
and belonging. Give yourself plenty of time to heal and recover. I recommend waiting a full four seasons before you make
any more major life changes. Ultimately you *will* end up in a
better situation.

There are three solutions to every
problem: accept it, change it or leave it.
If you can't accept it, change it.
If you can't change it, leave it. –Unknown

CHAPTER 4

Community Relationships

While the spirit of neighborliness was important on the frontier because neighbors were so few, it is even more important now because our neighbors are so many.

—Lady Bird Johnson

Community Relationships

Online life is so delicious because it is socializing with almost no friction.

—David Brooks

Community is not necessarily where we live, but where we belong. Our sense of connection and community has been steadily eroding. We moved from gathering with neighbors on our front porch to circling around the radio inside our living rooms. Family dinners devolved to eating on trays in front of the television. The internet has led to remote learning, virtual offices, online meetings and non-stop focus on our devices. While it seems like we are constantly connecting, loneliness, anxiety, depression, addiction, anger, suicide and violence have increased. In 2024 the World Happiness Report dropped the United States to 23rd overall and to 62nd for those under 30. Research proves we need in person human connection and a sense of belonging to lead emotionally and physically healthy lives. If we are going to better ourselves and society, we need to re-learn how to communicate and create an old-fashioned sense of community.

Reciprocity

Anyone who thinks that they are too small to make a difference

has never tried to fall asleep with a mosquito in the room.

—The Dalai Lama

To paraphrase former President Kennedy "Ask not what your community can do for you, but what you can do for your community." Know where and how to find your "people", your "tribe", your "fit". Where do you feel the most comfortable? Initiate connections with other like-minded souls. Find them in community centers, a meet-up, clubs, classes, conferences. If you are single, it is a great way to meet other singles in real life. One couple I know met at a gathering for tall people. Chat with other dog owners at the dog park. Volunteer. If you are an *introvert,* choose situations where you are involved, but with less interaction. Learn the *art of conversation* by asking simple questions such as: "What brought you here today?" "What do you do for enjoyment?" In this simple way, you are contributing to the betterment of society and yourself

Reliability

Definition of good neighbor: someone to be trusted; a courteous, friendly source of help when help is needed; someone you can count on; someone who cares.
−Edward B. Rust Jr.

Being a reliable, contributing or (at least non annoying) member of a community or neighborhood is another essential element of healthy relationships with other people. We can do simple things such as clean up our dog's poop, offer to share a walk, make soup, or even something more ambitious as starting a community garden. Maybe you bring refreshments to the neighborhood gathering, help build a stage for the town park, or organize a group outing or shopping trip. If you are putting yourself and your efforts out there in a way that benefits, and does not detract from your community, you are helping to create a better world and help yourself in the process. It's that simple.

Respect

Respect for ourselves guides our morals, respect for others

guides our manners.

−Laurence Sterne

Momentary interactions such as greeting and thanking others can increase wellbeing and a sense of belonging. Proving the adage that to give is better than to receive, it turns out that greeting strangers with a simple "good morning" and chatting with those we don't know can boost our own happiness. Some of the most heartwarming news stories are those where the garbage collector, delivery driver, or school crossing guard are being celebrated by a grateful and generous community. Being kind and taking time to notice and acknowledge those who make your life better is a sign of class and dignity. It is easy and it makes the world a better place.

Connecting Conversations in Community

The only way to truly know someone is by being with them,

by conversation.

— *Eric Overby*

One way to foster a sense of community and improve well-being is to gather three to five willing participants in a quiet place for the purpose of having deeper, more meaningful conversations. Think of it as a book club for connecting and this same book is used every time. Ask participants to choose something from the book that resonates - a quote, a chapter, a topic that they feel comfortable discussing. (This avoids digressing into complaint sessions.) Encourage participants to be a bit vulnerable and express from their heart. (See appendix). Each person talks for a minute or so while the others simply listen. Ask the speaker to solicit feedback if they wish, if not, let the others know they just wanted to feel heard. Encourage others to take a turn. Meet regularly - say monthly and see how much more deeply connected you feel after a few meetings.

Community Checklist

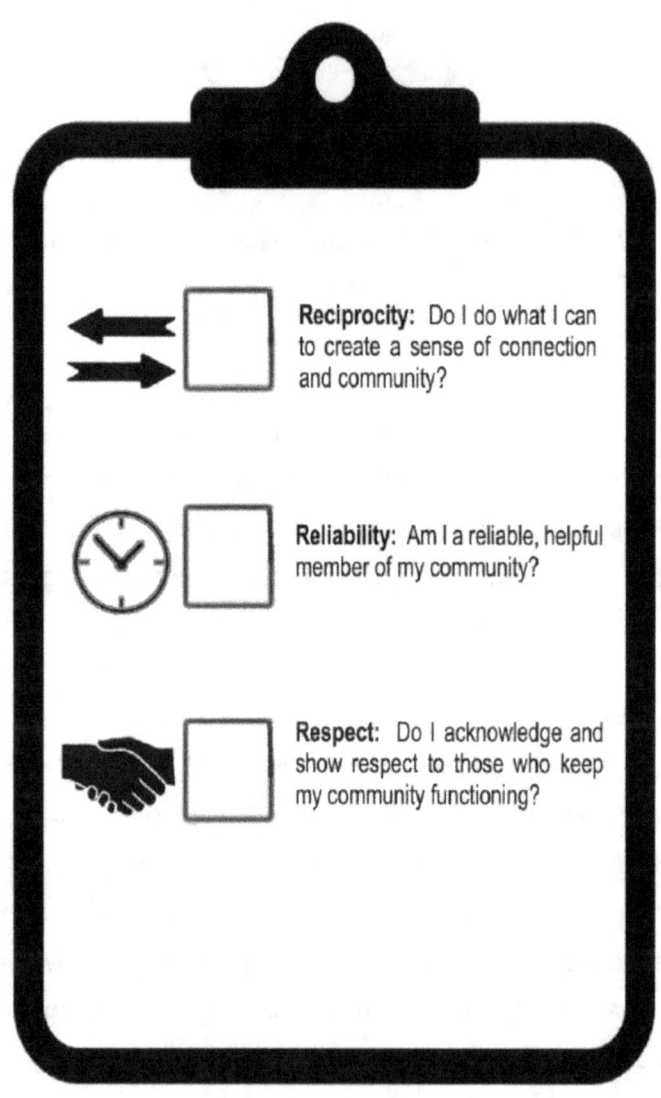

Reciprocity: Do I do what I can to create a sense of connection and community?

Reliability: Am I a reliable, helpful member of my community?

Respect: Do I acknowledge and show respect to those who keep my community functioning?

We live in a world in which we need to share responsibility. It's easy to say it's not my child, not my community, not my world, not my problem, then there are those who see the need and respond. I consider those people my heroes.
—Fred Rogers

CHAPTER 5

Social Relationships

Perhaps the most delightful friendships are those in which there is much agreement, much disputation, and yet more personal liking.

—George Eliot

Friendships

Yes'm, old friends is always best, 'less you can catch a new one that's fit to make an old one out of.

— Sarah Orne Jewett

Friendships change as we change, and friends often drift apart. We form our initial friendships based on proximity - the playmate next door. As we grow into adolescence, our friends are chosen based on shared attitudes, values, beliefs, interests and activities. When we reach adulthood, it is compatible lifestyles such as families, neighborhoods, and workplaces. Once we move into retirement, friendships change again - some endure, people move away or pass on. It can run the gamut from new and exciting to sad and painful. By being aware of the potential for change, and periodically reassessing, we can be prepared for the endings and still be grateful for the friendship that was.

Reciprocity

Friends are those rare people who ask how we are and then wait to

hear the answer.

—Ed Cunningham

Reciprocity of effort in friendship is basic. I initiate, you respond. You initiate, I respond. We take turns scheduling, planning, driving, hosting, buying, bringing, and sharing. We also take turns talking and listening and just being there. We try to connect regularly, ideally in real time. We share a meal or a walk as well as our troubles and our joys. It is special on a unique level that is not to be confused with social media acquaintances. When a friendship starts fading, the first place you will often notice it is reciprocity. They stop initiating. They slow down or stop responding. Or they make excuses. They cancel. If, after you have reached out for a connection three times with limited or no response, stop initiating. They may realize they have been neglecting the friendship and reach out. Or not.

Reliability

There's nothing like a really loyal, dependable, good friend. Nothing.

—Jennifer Aniston

Reliability is the friend you can count on. It is the friend that has your back. They show up when they say they will and do what they said they would do. I once overheard a young woman tearfully explaining: "My stupid friend never showed up and now I have to take a bus from Tacoma." It is the friend who checks on you when you don't answer, keeps an eye on your house when you are gone, or brings soup or a latte when you are down and out. When evaluating a friendship ask yourself: Is this someone I can count on? If not, and they have flaked out more than once or even twice, avoid any situation where you need to count on them. Three strikes? Out.

Respect

I've learned that people will forget what you said, people will forget what you did, but people will never forget how you made them feel.

—Maya Angelou

A friend respects your *boundaries* - when you say, "no thank you", they don't push the issue. They respect your confidences. When you say, "it's just between us", it remains "just between us". A friend may not agree with your values or beliefs, but when you "color outside the lines" they let it be. While good natured teasing is a part of friendship, they do not make snarky comments, take "pot shots" or ridicule. If they do, a snappy comeback might be: "Are you poking fun or just poking?" A friend respects your family and your partner - at least enough to lend a sympathetic ear and not disparage them in your presence. They respect you (and your finances) enough to modify where you go and what you do and what you eat and drink together and don't judge. In other words, in their presence, you feel safe, accepted and valued.

Friendship Checklist

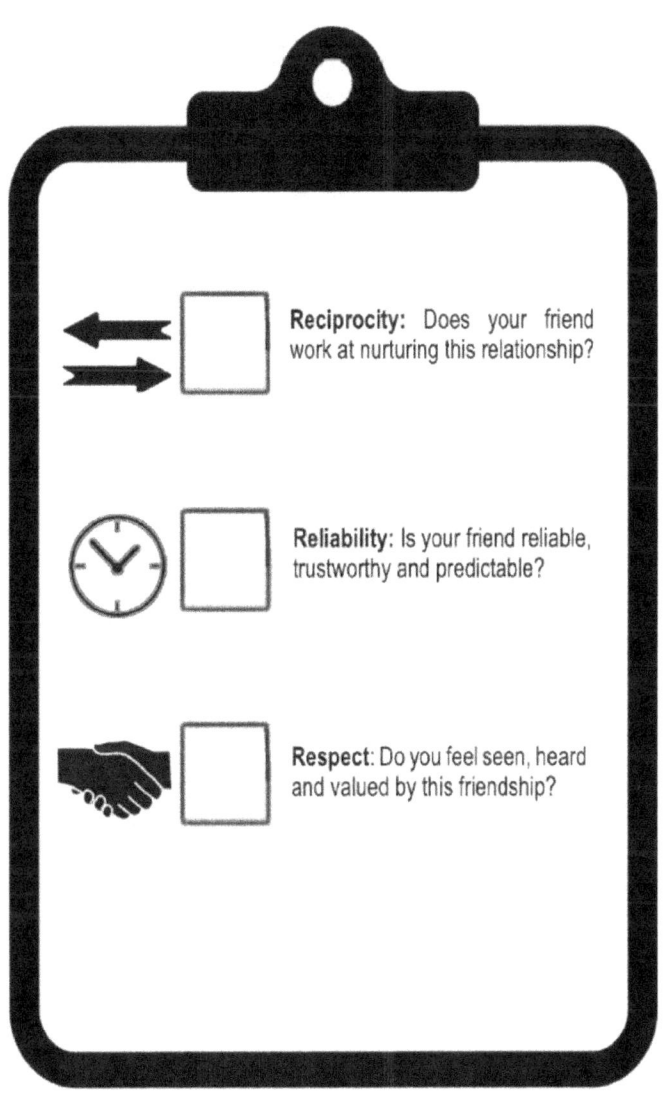

Reciprocity: Does your friend work at nurturing this relationship?

Reliability: Is your friend reliable, trustworthy and predictable?

Respect: Do you feel seen, heard and valued by this friendship?

Fun with Flags

If you feel drained after spending time with someone,

that's a red flag!

−Doreen Virtue

If you are questioning a friendship - maybe it is new and you are uncertain, or a longer-term friendship that seems to be fading, use the flags. Ask yourself the same sort of questions as you did on the checklist. If it is a friendship with a long history, do some reflection on your past times together. Have you been letting some things go out of habit or loyalty? Or have you not realized the good they have been contributing? Plant green, yellow and red flags accordingly. Step back and assess the results, then decide what to do.

Circles

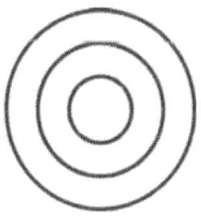

I have plenty of friends I don't like.

−Julian Fellows

At this point decide if this a one, two or three circle friendship. If less than three, what is workable, what you are willing to put up with? Social media without a face-to-face or real time connection? I would give it a one-circle relationship. Reciprocity and reliability may be enough for us as part of a shared activity such as a club or hobby – so give it a two-circle relationship. We may find we enjoy the company of someone with deeply shared values who is also a good listener, however their frustrating lack of reciprocity or reliability leaves us with a single circle association. When all three; reciprocity, reliability and respect are present, you have a good friend. Nurture the relationship.

Self-Reflection Friendship Checklist

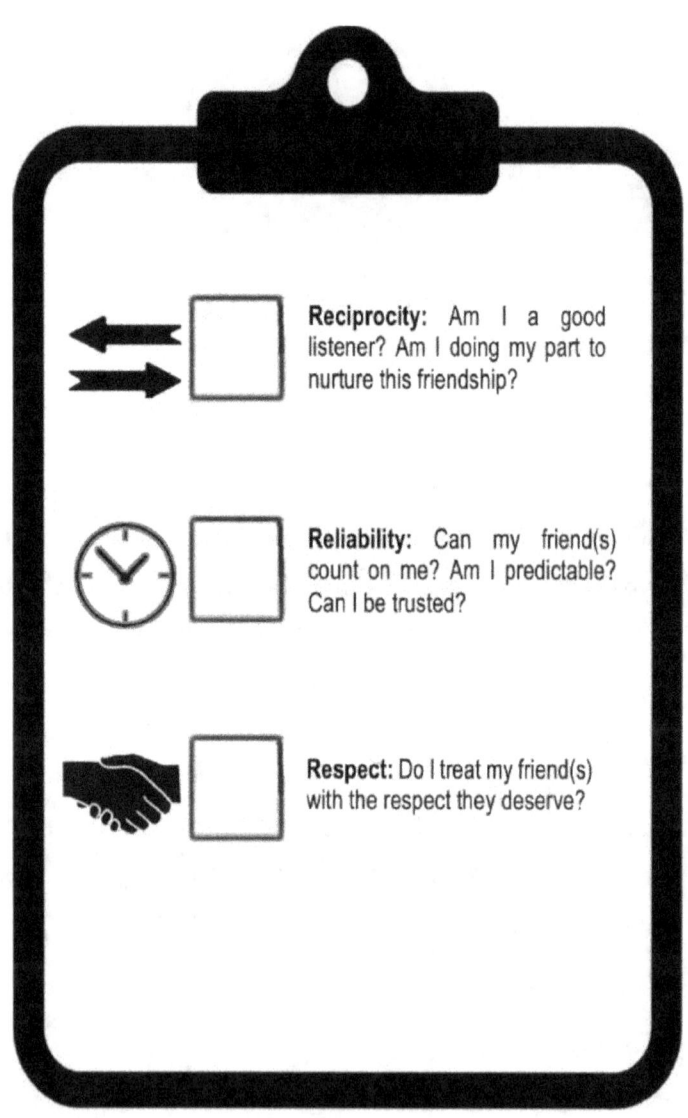

Reciprocity: Am I a good listener? Am I doing my part to nurture this friendship?

Reliability: Can my friend(s) count on me? Am I predictable? Can I be trusted?

Respect: Do I treat my friend(s) with the respect they deserve?

Solutions

Do Nothing Communicate Leave

When it is time to address issues in a friendship, your options come down to the same three potential solutions: *do nothing, communicate or leave.* Before you explore these options decide: Are you willing to fight for this friendship? Or could you let it go? While we hope for a win/win, we have no power unless we willing to risk losing. What else might you lose by ending this friendship? For example, is this friend part of a larger social circle or community you value? Is it more important *in this relationship* that you be liked or that you be respected? In friendships this is a double-edged sword: Of course, we want to be liked, but we don't want to be walked on or feel taken advantage of.

Do Nothing

People change and forget to tell each other.

−Lillian Hellman

Do not confuse doing nothing with lack of caring about the friendship. It's about keeping your self respect. When you stop initiating after three attempts, you are essentially doing nothing. You go on with life as if the friendship has ended. Although you might be hurt and confused, when you see them on the street, you wave hello. In other words, continue as if nothing has happened. Maybe they have their own "stuff" going on that you are unaware of. You might even have seen it coming when you realized your values were no longer aligned. Or maybe you have noticed signs of disconnecting such as rude behavior or distancing. Or they just stopped posting. Whatever. Shake your head and say: "It's their loss". By deliberately doing nothing you claim your power.

Communicate

I don't force friendships or communication. If its not mutual,
I'll let it go. It's that simple for me.
–Rob Hill Sr.

Current etiquette suggests about 24 to 48 hours for a response to texts. If you find yourself being ghosted and you value the friendship, you might reach out with: "Are we ok?" "Did I offend?" No response? There's your answer. They are dismissing your friendship. It's time to stop initiating. However, they may give you an opening such as: "Well, you made a few comments I didn't appreciate." They are saying the relationship is worth giving you the opportunity to make repairs. Be careful how you respond. Do not say "Sorry you felt that way". This is disrespecting their feelings and not taking ownership of your perceived offence. Instead, a simple, "I'm so sorry. I was an idiot. I did not mean to offend." You might try to explain your original intentions, however as the saying goes, "When you are in a hole, stop digging."

Leave

Sometimes you have to give up on people. Not because you don't care, but because they don't.

— Jennifer Green

If your friendship is draining you, or lacking more of the essentials than it is providing, it's time to let it go. Depending on the level of closeness, the loss of a friendship can be gut wrenching. Learn the process of grieving. After you have had time to recover, start reaching out to others. Maybe initially you just need someone else to fill that person's empty seat at your game table, sporting event, or team activity. Look to social groups that share your passions, activities or values and leave yourself open to forming new friendships. Like a threadbare comforter that is no longer comforting, it might be time to give it up and find a new one.

Friendship Solutions Checklist

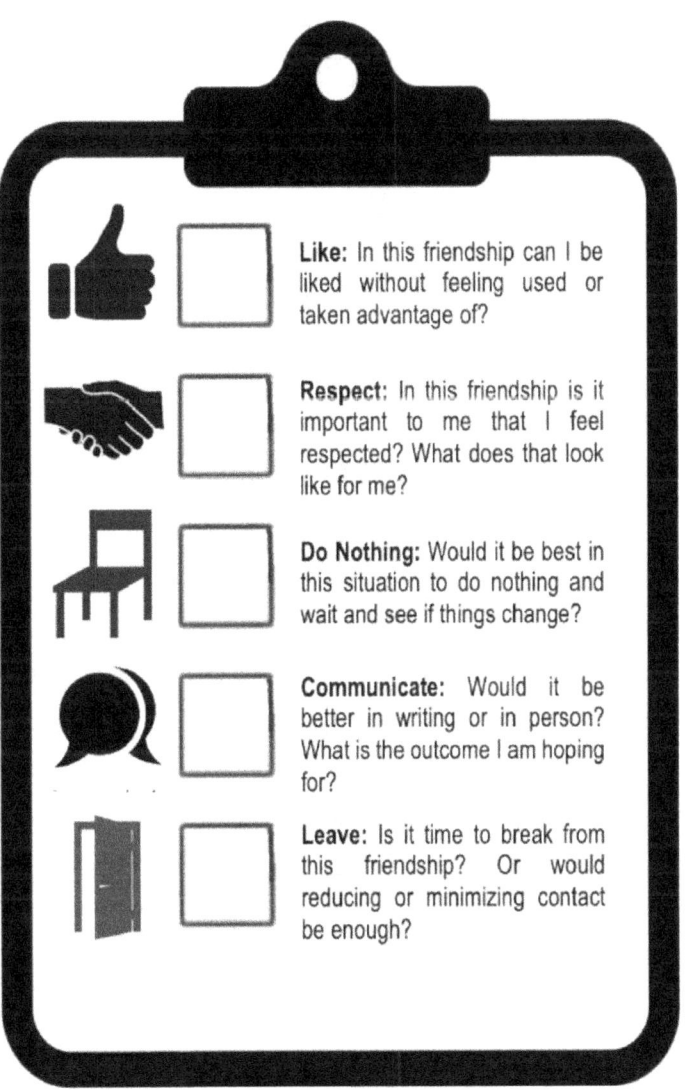

Like: In this friendship can I be liked without feeling used or taken advantage of?

Respect: In this friendship is it important to me that I feel respected? What does that look like for me?

Do Nothing: Would it be best in this situation to do nothing and wait and see if things change?

Communicate: Would it be better in writing or in person? What is the outcome I am hoping for?

Leave: Is it time to break from this friendship? Or would reducing or minimizing contact be enough?

Connected Conversations with Friends

A friend is a person with whom I may be honest. Before him, I may

think aloud.

—Ralph Waldo Emerson

To initiate a deeper conversation with a friend, find a quiet place and sit down. You cannot connect well while in constant motion, looking at devices, or in a noisy environment. Set the tone by saying, "I need to talk about something, would you mind just listening for a moment?" Then express yourself simply, straight from your heart. An example might be "I'm really worried that I won't be able to make this new project work. I've paid a lot of money; I might have just made a big mistake." If they are a good listener, they will sit quietly, giving you an opportunity to say more, or echo your concern with an "oh my, that is worrisome" or even encourage you to dig deeper by asking "what is your worst fear"? If however, they seem uncomfortable or barrage you with unsolicited advice they have not yet learned how to deeply connect.

Friendship is the hardest thing in the world to explain. It's not something you learn in school. But if you haven't learned the meaning of friendship, you really haven't learned anything.

–Muhammad Ali

CHAPTER 6

Professional Relationships

Enjoy your achievements as well as your plans. Keep
interested in your own career, however humble; it is a
real possession in the changing fortunes of time.

−Max Ehrmann

Professional Relationships

I hold a little fundraiser every day. It's called going to work.

— *Stephen Colbert*

Most of us work. As an Employee Assistance Provider (EAP), I often do work-related confidential counseling. I find the number one concern expressed by clients is dealing with other people. It might be the passive-aggressive coworker, the snarky colleague, the micromanaging supervisor or an incompetent, unappreciative boss. Then there is the oh so subtle sexual harasser flying just under the radar, or the co-worker who manages to stick you with all the work while they take the credit. It's frustrating. While quitting is an option, there are always going to be other people challenges and we may as well figure out what they are and how to deal with them.

Reciprocity

Hard work spotlights the character of people: some turn up their sleeves, some turn up their noses, and some don't turn up at all.

—Sam Ewing

Are you doing most of the heavy lifting? Reciprocity of effort is what makes the world of work, work. It's the essence of building positive professional relationships and encouraging cooperation. Simple enough, right? We expect reciprocity in getting the job done. There are also those small subtleties that are "not in the job description" such as a cheerful "good morning", the offer to bring the pastries or refilling the coffee maker even when no one is looking. More powerful is the simple "thank you" or "well done" to a colleague or a subordinate. This kind of reciprocity costs nothing, yet these are the little things that can make or break a work environment.

Reliability

If I made a commitment, I stood by that commitment - and try to make it real...the most important thing you have is your word, your trust.
−Michelle Obama

Reliability and predictability at work. How can anyone *not* be reliable and still have a job? It is baffling. Yet time and again, you see the chronically late, the frequently ill, or the burned-out senior co-worker who just doesn't care anymore. Beware of the *sociopathic* saboteur who leaves you holding the bag while throwing you under the bus. They are often charismatic charmers who believe winning is more important than anything or anyone. They instinctively know how to appeal to fears and weakness. Ultimately, they can take down individuals, companies and even countries. It's a very tough position to find yourself in and more common than most people realize.

Respect

The whole concept of treating people with dignity and respect is a concept that isn't a business concept, it's a life concept.

−Greg Brenneman

According to a Pew study, 57% of Americans quit their jobs because they felt disrespected at work. But what exactly does respect look and feel like? Is it formal recognition - the employee of the month parking spot? For most, it's being seen and feeling heard. It's a sense of being valued as a human being and for your contribution, no matter how small. It's being treated kindly, and it is just plain good manners. A client said to me: "I love my CEO, he acknowledges everyone, the security guard, the cleaning staff, the receptionist. He exemplifies work life balance and values. I've seen him turn down a state dinner to be at his daughter's school play. It makes me want to do whatever I can to help him, and our company succeed." This begs the question; what is so hard about showing respect?

Professional Relationships Checklist

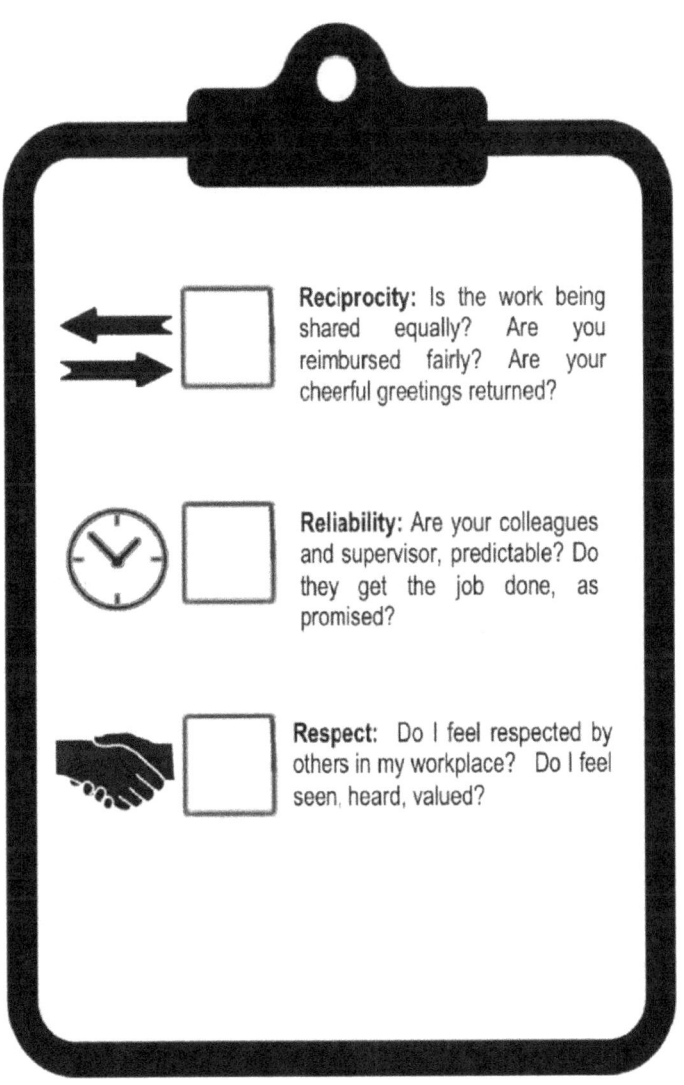

Reciprocity: Is the work being shared equally? Are you reimbursed fairly? Are your cheerful greetings returned?

Reliability: Are your colleagues and supervisor, predictable? Do they get the job done, as promised?

Respect: Do I feel respected by others in my workplace? Do I feel seen, heard, valued?

Flags

When a workplace becomes toxic its poison spreads beyond its
walls and into the lives of its workers and their families
−Gary Chapman

Planting flags is a way of giving us a sense of control and is less creepy than poking pins in a Voodoo doll. If necessary, disguise your flag display as a pen holder and keep it on your desk. Keep an ample supply of flags in a desk drawer. When they happen, note positive interactions with others and plant green flags generously. Toss in yellow flags if uncertain. Plant red flags as needed for those obviously negative situations. Simply note, over time, how that display is coming along. More green than yellow or red? Appreciate what you have. More yellow? Figure out what you can do to move it to green. Is there more red than any other color? Time to regroup....

Circles

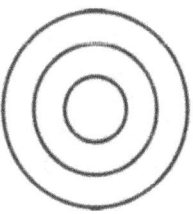

The stronger your inner circle, the more opportunities will be presented to you.

–Ryan Malinowski

At this point it is time to decide is this a one, two or three circle job or career. If less than three, decide what is workable and what you are willing to put up with. Maybe you have an easy commute, or they are generous when you need time off to take care of a sick child. Maybe you feel emotionally valued, but grossly underpaid. Give it two-circles. Or you are being paid an extraordinary amount but have been relocated to someplace you find miserable. Or you and your boss do not speak the same language - literally or figuratively. It may be a one circle situation. You decide if you can manage it - at least for the short term. Visualizing the limitations via circles is another way to come to terms with a situation.

Self-Reflection Professional Checklist

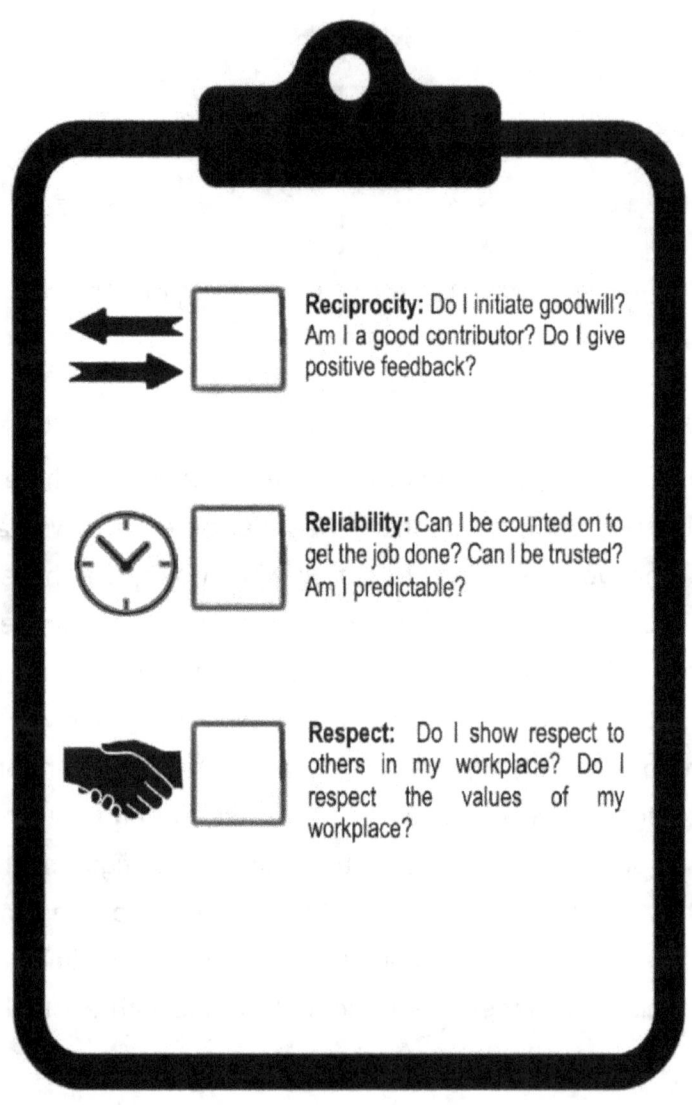

Reciprocity: Do I initiate goodwill? Am I a good contributor? Do I give positive feedback?

Reliability: Can I be counted on to get the job done? Can I be trusted? Am I predictable?

Respect: Do I show respect to others in my workplace? Do I respect the values of my workplace?

Solutions

When it is time to evaluate your professional options, it comes down once again, to the three potential solutions: *do nothing, communicate* or *leave*. Are you willing to fight for yourself in this situation? While we hope for a win/win, we have no power unless we are willing to risk losing. Giving up a job or career is not to be taken lightly. In addition, when it comes to professional situations, it is usually more important that you be respected. This means first, identify what you want. Is it a raise? Respect? Feedback? Corner office? Time off? What are your expectations? Are you willing to compromise? Whatever it is, communicate briefly, assertively and directly.

Do Nothing

Life was always a matter of waiting for the right moment to act.

−Paulo Coelho

Choosing to do nothing while you watch and wait things out may be the most prudent in a work environment. Hopefully, you have used your tools, and you have a solid idea of what you are dealing with. What needs to change for things to improve? How long can you emotionally afford to wait things out? Can you make a commitment to do nothing for three months? Six months? A year? Take a breather. Committing to doing nothing and accepting the situation as is may be more freeing than you thought.

Communicate

We don't get what we deserve. We get what we believe we deserve.

–Don Cooper

Being a good communicator is an acquired skill and most of us do not do well with it under pressure. In general: Decide in advance what you want to accomplish. Then ask for what you want. Be specific. Keep it short and simple. Determine if it is best to do in person or in writing. Understand the differences in the following communication styles: *Passive* is apologetic and tentative; sentences tend to end with a question mark. *Assertive* is direct but not offensive and sentences end with a period. *Aggressive* comes across as critical or angry and sentences might be written in all capital letters and/or end with an exclamation point. Strive for assertive. Be prepared to handle those *passive-aggressive* sabotaging snipers. They tend to be subtle, indirect and snarky. Response is best handled by calling them out with this snappy comeback: "Are you trying to be helpful or hurtful?"

Leave

What would you do if you weren't afraid?
−David Brooks

When you are on the edge about leaving your position, or considering a new assignment or endeavor, ask yourself: What do I really want? A client struggling with career questions responded clearly with: "I want to make beautiful things with my hands." Try on your dreams and ideas. Ask yourself if you could be comfortable as an entrepreneur with autonomy but no security. Consider phasing gradually by while keeping security and benefits. Want to open your own restaurant? Visit potential space and imagine what your place would look like. Prefer the benefits and opportunities of a large corporation? Make connections, get out, let people know you are available. When you are ready, you will know what to do. Commitment sets you free.

Professional Solutions Checklist

Like: Is it important for me to be liked in this situation?

Respect: Is it important for me to be respected in this situation?

Do Nothing: Is there a benefit to doing nothing for now and see if things change?

Communicate: What *do* I want? Is it time to communicate assertively and asking for what I want?

Leave: Is it time to move on? What is it I *really* want to be doing?

Connected Conversations at Work

Vulnerability sounds like truth and feels like courage. Truth and

courage are not always comfortable, but they're never

weaknesses.

—Brene' Brown

When it comes to deeper connections and shared vulnerabilities at work, what are the unspoken rules? I was a brand-new affiliate psychology professor on my way to my first class when, in passing, the Dean of Instruction asked me: "How are you feeling about your new class?" I replied: "Insecure and overwhelmed." She stopped dead in her tracks saying: "Oh my, we all feel that way, but no one ever actually *says* it." To this day, I'm not sure if I had just done a good thing or a bad thing. What were the rules? What I can say is that whenever I have had a brief water cooler style conversation about a vulnerability - usually with another colleague in my building, I felt much less isolated. This begs the question of those who establish the cultural norms at work - how do *you* encourage safe, open, honest, connected conversations?

No one who achieves success does so
without acknowledging the help of others.
The wise and confident acknowledge /
this help with gratitude.
— Alfred North Whitehead

CHAPTER 7

Family Relationships

Happy families are alike; every unhappy family

is unhappy in its own way.

–Leo Tolstoy

Family Relationships

Home is the place where if you have to go there
they have to take you in.
−Robert Frost

Home should be a safe, soft place to land. For this to work, families must be accountable to the same three essentials - reciprocity, reliability and respect as anyone else. Yet we excuse bad behavior because "it's family". Society and religion often condone or ignore ill treatment because we have been taught that families are sacred. "Honor thy father and thy mother". "Blood is thicker than water." Yet even the Bible acknowledges family dysfunction: "And a person's enemies will be those of his own household." (Matthew 10:36.) Families are essential to our survival from birth. Without them, we would die. On some level we are always aware of this, which is why we continue to seek acceptance and connection. This is fine if the family is nurturing. When it is not, it can be demoralizing, debilitating and often impacts all our other relationships.

Reciprocity

Someone can love you deeply, but if they don't have
the emotional skills to care for the relationship,
it will be a rough road.
– Yung Pueblo

In families we tend to do what we do because it is what we have always done - even when it is not working. When you break it down, reciprocity is basic. I initiate, you respond. You initiate, I respond. We all contribute in some way or another to family gatherings. More importantly, we work at just being there for one another. We show interest in each other's lives. We try to connect deeply. But what if your family's connection style is more like trying to get water from an empty well? To a request for more connection from my family, I received this reply: "Why do we need to keep in touch? You can see what I'm doing on social media." In this case, the rules of engagement have been clearly established and reciprocity of effort is not a priority.

Reliability

The worst thing in life is to end up with people that make you

feel all alone.

−Robin Williams

Reliability is the essence that family is founded upon. We are born helpless and dependent. If the family is predictable and reliable, we can become healthy functioning adults. If not, we tend to develop insecure *attachment styles.* This is the theory that the way we bond with our parental caregivers affects how we attach to others in our adult life. There is nothing more heartbreaking than a little boy waiting, and waiting, for his absentee father on visitation day. Or a little girl alone on the curb outside of school waiting for her mother who forgot her again. Sadly, a child cannot easily change their circumstances. In adulthood however, if there is still a family tendency toward lack of reliability, we can make informed choices. Like Charlie Brown *not* kicking the football held by Lucy, we can learn to avoid those situations.

Respect

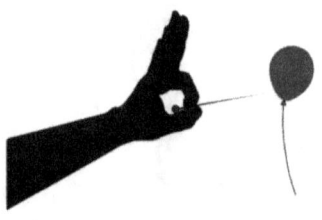

Family is supposed to be our safe haven. Very often, it's the place
we find the deepest heartache.

−Iyanla Vansant

Respect means non-violation and families can be the place we feel most violated. This can run the gamut from inattentive, distant or neglectful to being verbally, physically and/or sexually abusive. This can stem from a lack of awareness to loss of control, mental health issues, substance abuse and/or being just plain evil. Definitions of family systems can range from healthy and normal to eccentric or dysfunctional and even toxic. As a result, we may be acting out our preassigned *family roles* such as *hero, mascot, lost child* or *scapegoat*. Whatever the case, if our sense of self is suffering, if we feel we are not good enough, or believe we are damaged goods, we need to take an honest look at our family system. The pain will not go away, but we can learn to make it more comfortable and experience remarkable personal growth in the process.

Family Relationship Checklist

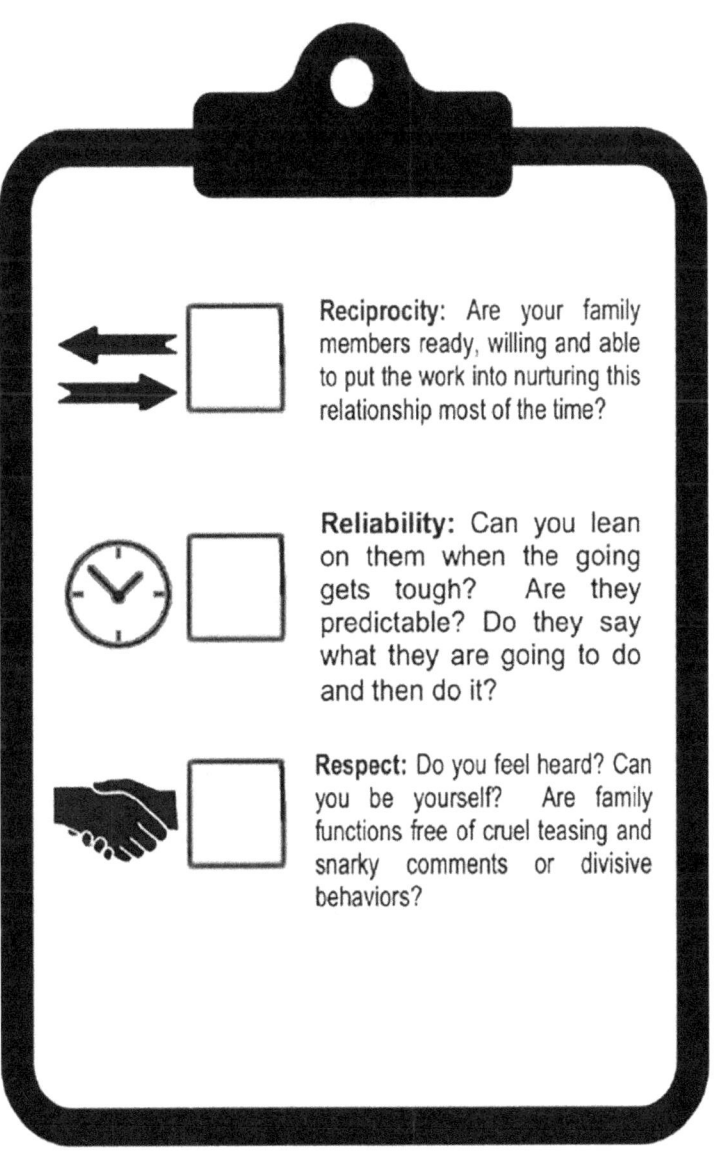

Reciprocity: Are your family members ready, willing and able to put the work into nurturing this relationship most of the time?

Reliability: Can you lean on them when the going gets tough? Are they predictable? Do they say what they are going to do and then do it?

Respect: Do you feel heard? Can you be yourself? Are family functions free of cruel teasing and snarky comments or divisive behaviors?

Fun with Flags

The longer we ignore red flags, pretend they don't exist, the more

we disconnect from ourselves.

−Sherrie Campbell

If you are questioning a family relationship, especially if you are at the point of debating a reduction in contact or even cut-off, try the flags. Pull from your memories and start planting. It might be uncomfortable. Be fair. Plant green ones for those good times. Not sure, yellow. Have plenty of red flags on hand for those past painful situations. This is not to encourage keeping grudges, but to prevent you from going back into a situation that may not be good for your well-being. If you end up with a display with more green and yellow, than hooray - it is not as bad as you thought. If you have more than a few red flags, stop initiating and limit contact.

Circles

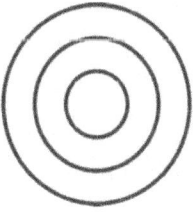

There are patterns which emerge in one's life, circling and returning

anew, an endless variation of a theme.

— Jacqueline Carey

At this point you might want to decide - is this a one, two or three circle family. If less than three, decide what is workable, and what you are willing to put up with. The obligatory phone call on birthdays? – If that is enough for you, give it a one-circle relationship. Reciprocity and reliability may be enough for us as part of family gatherings, but we find their values repugnant. In this case, give it a two-circle relationship. We may find we enjoy their company, but their lack of reciprocity or reliability leaves us with just more heartache. It's another visual way to encourage a level of acceptance. Or not.

Self Reflection Family Checklist

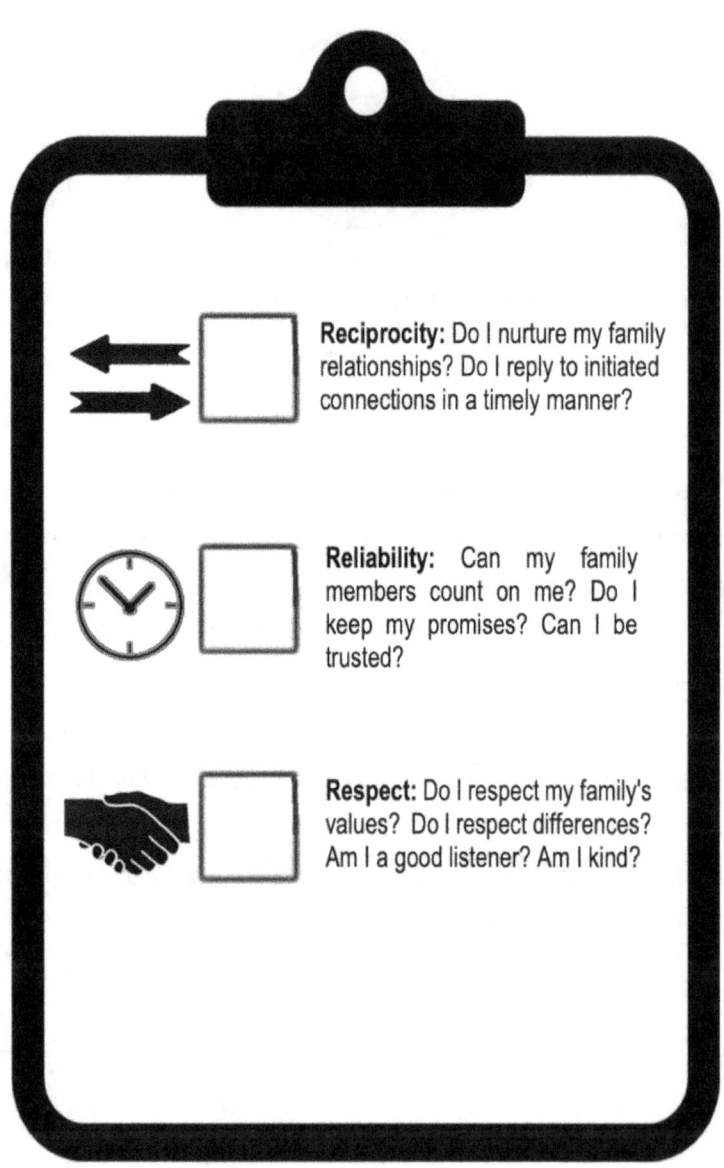

Reciprocity: Do I nurture my family relationships? Do I reply to initiated connections in a timely manner?

Reliability: Can my family members count on me? Do I keep my promises? Can I be trusted?

Respect: Do I respect my family's values? Do I respect differences? Am I a good listener? Am I kind?

Solutions

Do Nothing Communicate Leave

When it is time to address issues in a family system, your options come down the three potential solutions. Before you decide, are you willing to fight for this family? Or could you let it go? While we hope for a win/win, we have no power unless we are willing to risk losing, and losing family is traumatic. If it is toxic, you have much to think about. Is it more important in this family that you be liked or that you be respected? When we want to be liked we can be taken advantage of. When we want to be respected, we protect ourselves, but risk negative pushback. Respect also means setting firm boundaries. Be prepared - this may be such a change in how the system normally functions the family may double down their efforts to maintain the status quo.

Do Nothing

The problem with doing nothing is you never know when

you are finished.

—Groucho Marx

Deliberately choosing to do nothing is about reassessing. When you stop reaching out or responding to negative interactions, you are keeping your self-respect and your power. You can take a break from family. You learn to stop hoping for connection, predictability, respect. You go on with your life. You stop trying to get water from an empty well. At some point, the family may realize you have distanced and begin reaching out to you - especially if your role in the family is essential for them to maintain the status quo. If it is genuine and a sincere effort, take advantage of the opportunity to make repairs. Be cautious, it might be only a token effort. Like a slot machine, *intermittent reinforcement* can keep you hooked.

Communicate

You can't reason someone out of something that they weren't reasoned into in the first place.

–Mark Twain

To improve the family interactions, you might start with a simple greeting card or meme indicating your openness. It is testing the water before a potentially difficult and volatile conversation. Or reach out with: 'Can we talk?' Use "I feel" statements. "When you exclude me, I feel hurt". "When you no showed for my graduation, I felt let down." "I wish we had a stronger connection." You get the idea. Make sure your side of the street is clean - no accusations, no nastiness. Give them a chance to apologize, "make nice" or try to save face. Then take a breather and see where it goes. Kudos to the parent or sibling who listens openly. There is hope. If they dismiss your concerns and respond with denying, negative, discrediting, or toxic statements, pull back. They are not yet ready to change their long-standing point of view.

Leave

The path to freedom is illuminated by the bridges you have burned,
adorned by the ties you have cut, and cleared by the drama you
have left behind.
−Steve Maraboli

If your family is lacking more of the essentials than it is providing, or worse, is toxic and painful for you, it is time to formulate a plan. Start with something I call "ritualized cutoff". You pull back from family interactions - not so far that they notice, just far enough to keep yourself sane and safe. It is also a way to keep from feeling too much guilt over your decision. You show up twice a year, maybe a birthday or holiday. You stay two hours. Think of it as the "rule of twos". It is a way to leave without going so far as complete cutoff. It can work if you are no longer vulnerable or invested. However, if even limited interactions feel toxic and painful then family estrangement may be your only recourse. Before you decide on this step, professional help might be in order.

Family Solutions Checklist

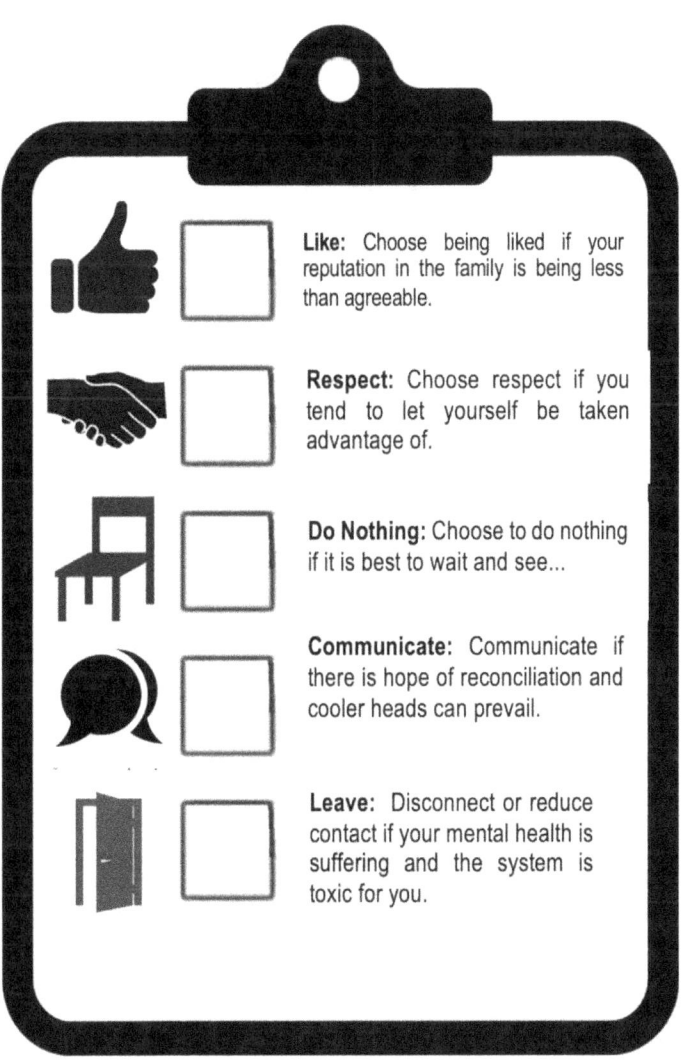

Like: Choose being liked if your reputation in the family is being less than agreeable.

Respect: Choose respect if you tend to let yourself be taken advantage of.

Do Nothing: Choose to do nothing if it is best to wait and see...

Communicate: Communicate if there is hope of reconciliation and cooler heads can prevail.

Leave: Disconnect or reduce contact if your mental health is suffering and the system is toxic for you.

Connecting Conversations in Family

Rules without relationship equals rebellion

— Josh McDowell

Modern families are often a disconnected, discombobulated mess - isolated on devices, overworked parents with over-scheduled kids often with limited resources. They may be powder kegs ready to blow. Sometimes it is the acting out adolescent who is desperately trying to send a misunderstood plea for help. Slowing it all down and creating regular opportunities for deeper connections can go a long way to creating healthier families. Share at least one device free meal per week. Although your adolescent will resist, ask them open ended questions. Have the littlest ones contribute dinner table topics. You might be surprised at just how perceptive a five-year-old can be - they were often my best ally in family therapy sessions. Encourage nonjudgmental sharing of emotions by using drawing cards of feeling emojis or cutouts from the faces in the movie Inside Out. Strictly adhere to a five-minute listen only rule - parents, this means you too.

Feelings of worth can flourish only in an /
atmosphere where individual differences are
appreciated, mistakes are tolerated,
communication is open, and rules are flexible
- the kind of atmosphere that is found in a
nurturing family. –Virginia Satir

CHAPTER 8

Romantic Relationships

We want one person to give us companionship, economic

support, co-parenting, intellectual equal, best friend,

confidant, passionate lover — and we also hope to

find that person on an app.

–Esther Perel

Romantic Relationships

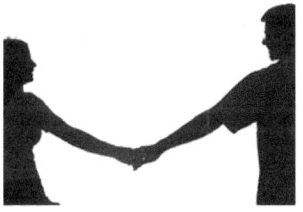

The strongest relationships are between two people who can live without each other but don't want to.

−Harriet Lerner

Romantic relationships are tricky because we humans are vulnerable and there is more risk of deep emotional hurt. Keeping our eyes open and honestly assessing may prevent some of the heartache later. For a romantic relationship to be viable, it should contain at least the three essentials − *reciprocity of effort, reliability of commitment and respect for values*, most of the time. If the relationship is to progress to another level and deepen, add *passion, intimacy and commitment.* Keeping up is like playing the old carnival game of "Whack a Mole". As soon as you have one essential figured out, another one needing attention pops up. Before you get overwhelmed, remember, relationships are always a work in progress.

Reciprocity

A lack of reciprocity in a relationship isn't an invitation for you to try to convince them of your worth.

—Helena Hart

Reciprocity of effort in a romantic relationship means both parties work to nurture the health of their relationship. To this end they find *rituals for connection* and learn each other's *love languages.* They contribute equally, on balance, to create a shared world. This includes an agreed-upon frequency and means of checking in with each other. It is also demonstrating your appreciation and showing good manners. We need to regularly express gratitude for even the smallest of our partner's contributions. It is also a willingness to take part and/or support the activities and interests of the other. It means to engage together with family and friends. It also means sharing financial resources – while that may not always be equitable, it works if the limits are understood. When reciprocity is missing, the relationship can derail.

Reliability

Trust is not built in big, sweeping moments. It's built in tiny moments every day.

–Brene' Brown

Reliability in intimate relationships is a cornerstone that speaks to our most primal concerns – safety and security. When a partner says he or she will, and they do not, it imperceptibly affects our sense of well-being and subtly erodes the foundation of the relationship. This is why those seemingly benign issues such as household chores become monumental. Predictability and consistency of behavior also fall under reliability. These can become serious challenges, when unkept promises of change are critical. While not *always* fatal to the relationship, the more serious issues of faithfulness and dishonesty can cause serious damage. Reliability means dependability - can I count on you - today, tomorrow, forever?

Respect

We don't need to share the same opinions as others, but we need to be respectful.

—*Taylor Swift*

Respect means taking into consideration the feelings, needs, thoughts, beliefs, wishes, boundaries, preferences, individual style and idosyncracies of the other. While this is a very big ask, it is critical to the health of a relationship. Much as we would like to, we cannot change the basic personality traits of the other. One of you may be an introverted homebody while the other a social butterfly. One of you is frugal, the other a spendthrift. One a neatnick, the other messy. Ultimately, what can you live with? We learn to compromise or navigate around the differences rather than fight the losing battle to change each other. Otherwise, lack of respect can lead to disdain and contempt, and we run the risk of destroying our relationship.

Three More Essentials

In order for a relationship to flourish, three more essentials must be added to the mix: *passion, intimacy and commitment.* As a couple's therapist I begin a session with "What is working"? Their spontaneous answers reveal a great deal. I listen and watch for the first three, *reciprocity, reliability and respect.* I am also listening for hints of shared passion(s), watching for emotional intimacy and parsing out a language of commitment. The next question: "What is not working?" usually tells the rest of the story. I use all six as a baseline in my head. It is an approach that you can try on your own to narrow down a more specific are of concern.

Passion

Don't pass up a chance by dumping someone after a first date because you don't feel the fireworks. The fireworks can happen at any time and be maintained.

−Helen Fisher

Passion involves feelings and desires that lead to physical attraction, romance, and sexual consummation. After the initial fireworks, it can morph into shared enthusiasms such as interests and activities. We often hear it said that there is just "no spark". "Spark" is brain chemistry that often leads to trouble - dubious one-night stands, extramarital affairs, a regretful trip to the Elvis Chapel. It is the equivalent of putting your finger in a light socket. You get one helluva charge, but it is not such a good idea. On the other hand, since the mundane is a passion killer, couples must work to create and keep "spark", and it will look different for everyone.

Intimacy

Intimacy is not purely physical. It's the act of connecting with someone so deeply, you feel like you can see into their soul.

—Reshall Varsos

It is a classic couple's issue. One wants to just be heard, the other wants to fix the problem. Learn to say: "I don't need you to fix this, I just need you to listen." It is an ongoing dilemma - do I offer practical advice or emotional support? Learn to ask: "What can I do to help?" or "Do you want to be heard, helped or hugged?" It is especially difficult when we see a clear and obvious solution to a problem. This is comically demonstrated in a short You Tube video titled: "It's Not About the Nail". We need to trust that the other person will figure out what they need to do once their feelings have been validated. It is awkward at first, yet it is precisely this *active listening* skill that leads to emotional intimacy, flourishing conversations, and a much stronger couple bond.

Commitment

I hope we'll get lucky enough to grow old together.

— *Paula Mclain*

Commitment is not about the formal ceremony. It is an emotional investment in your future together. I believe it begins when your toothbrushes start sharing the same holder. It is a frame of mind and if it is not there, why waste the time and energy? A young man brought his fiancé' "bridezilla" to my office for premarital counseling. Five minutes into our initial session she stomped out on her stilettos, saying "I don't have time for this relationship s**t, I have a wedding to plan". That about said it all. While we often move too quickly to end a relationship when the going gets tough, in this case, I found myself hoping he would become a runaway bridegroom. It only took one statement and five minutes to see that commitment and most of the other essentials were missing.

Relationship Checklist

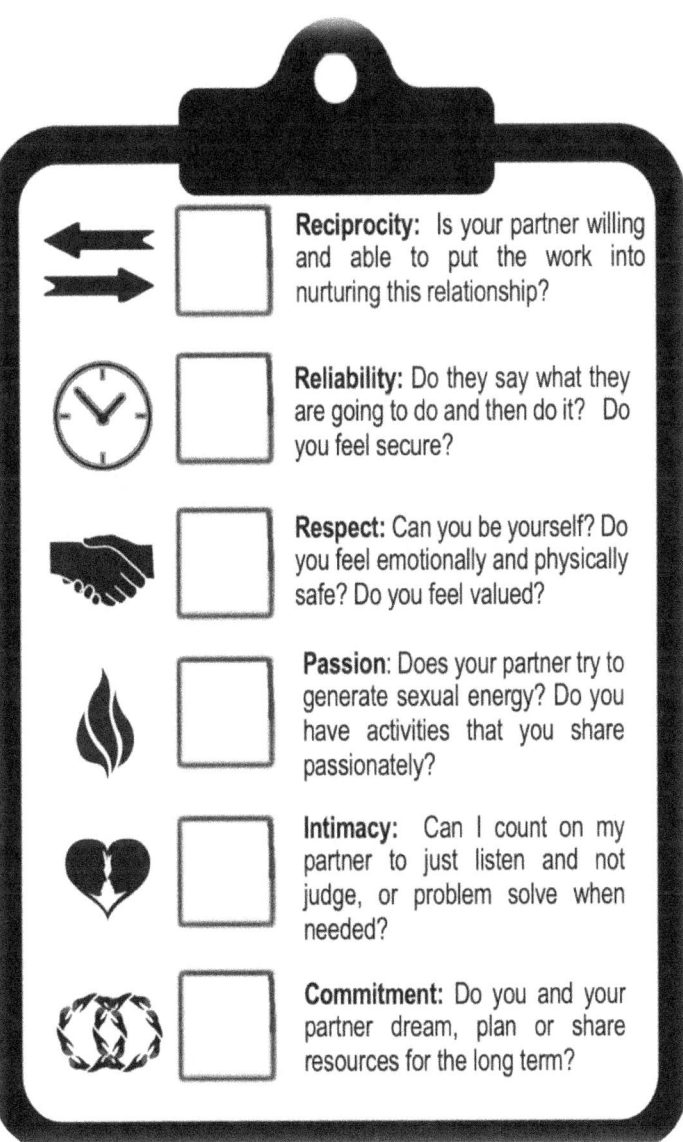

Reciprocity: Is your partner willing and able to put the work into nurturing this relationship?

Reliability: Do they say what they are going to do and then do it? Do you feel secure?

Respect: Can you be yourself? Do you feel emotionally and physically safe? Do you feel valued?

Passion: Does your partner try to generate sexual energy? Do you have activities that you share passionately?

Intimacy: Can I count on my partner to just listen and not judge, or problem solve when needed?

Commitment: Do you and your partner dream, plan or share resources for the long term?

Fun with Flags

I wish the pain of betrayal was as easy to ignore as the red flags

that forewarned of it.

—Steve Maraboli

This is a good place to stop and assess your relationship. Be brutally honest. What is working? What is not working? (What about bringing your flag display on dates? Just kidding. Is there an app for this?) Add in more flags as you spend time together. Once you have a good visual, you should begin to see a pattern and can make an informed decision about the future. Fun fact: When you ask someone later, as they are exiting a relationship, they will often admit they saw, but chose to ignore the red flags. Save yourself future heartache. Be on alert for indications of behaviors that are *toxic* for you - and vigilantly watch for the three R's - *reciprocity of effort, reliability of commitment and respect for values.*

Circles

Our lives are long, and our circles are small...Right relationship is knowing that we are interconnected and finding a form of connection that allows us peace.

—Valarie Kaur

Romantic relationships can range from "chaste courting", "just dating", "friends with benefits", "booty calls", being an "item", "living with" to long term committed and/or married. How would you describe yours at this point? Then assess based on the six essentials: *reciprocity, reliability, respect, passion, intimacy, and commitment.* You might decide this is currently just a one or two circle relationship and it is just fine for now. If you want something more, I suggest looking for at least the first three essentials. Something serious should be at least a four, working toward a five, even a six-circle relationship. If less than three, decide what is workable, what you are willing to work for and check back in the future.

Self Reflection Relationship Checklist

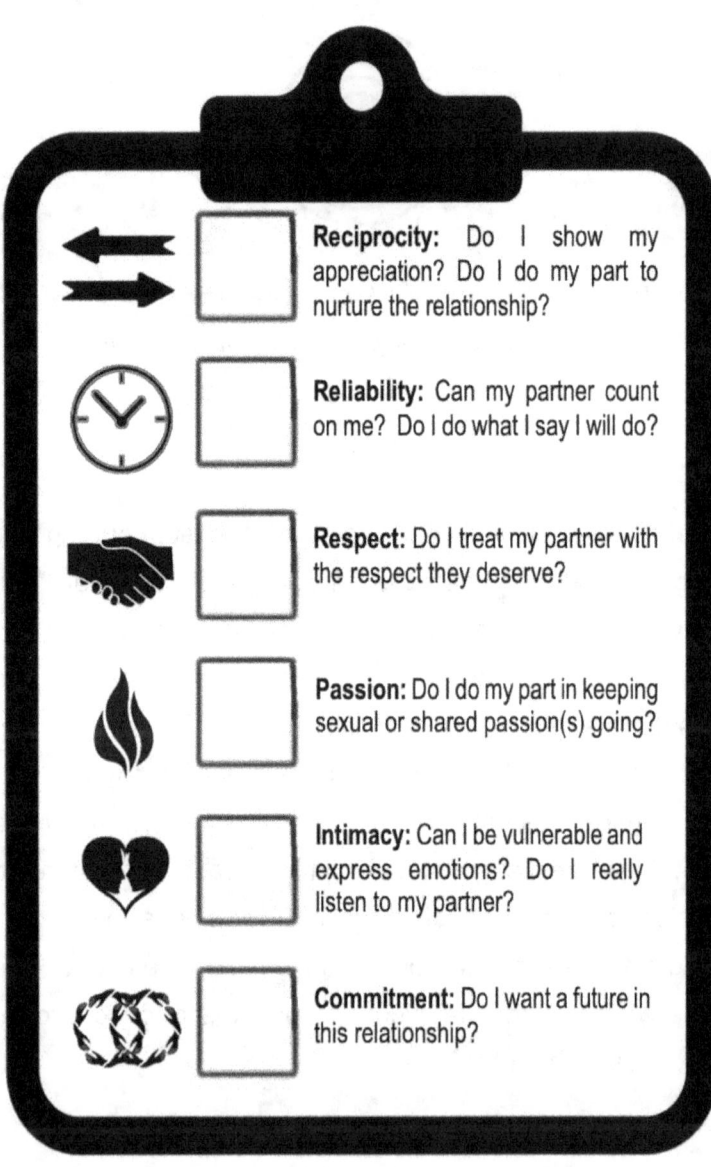

Reciprocity: Do I show my appreciation? Do I do my part to nurture the relationship?

Reliability: Can my partner count on me? Do I do what I say I will do?

Respect: Do I treat my partner with the respect they deserve?

Passion: Do I do my part in keeping sexual or shared passion(s) going?

Intimacy: Can I be vulnerable and express emotions? Do I really listen to my partner?

Commitment: Do I want a future in this relationship?

Solutions

When it is time to address issues in your relationship, your options come down to the three potential solutions: *do nothing, communicate or leave.* Stretch yourself. If you normally do nothing, communicate. If you are the type to cut and run, sit still. If you are one to verbally let loose, sit still or walk away. Also ask: "Is it more important that I be loved or that I be respected?" When we want to be loved, we tend to be over accommodating and "nice". While it may seem easier, in the long run it can invite contempt. When we want to be respected, we tend to ask for what we want, and set clear boundaries. Initially it might seem like you could be creating emotional distance, but in the longer run, respect for yourself leads to greater closeness.

Do Nothing

While you'll feel compelled to charge forward it's often a gentle step back
that will reveal to you where you and what you truly seek.
—Rasheed Ogunlaru

Do not confuse doing nothing with *passivity*. There is power in not responding and moments where silence is truly golden. When it looks like a situation is escalating and you are at risk of losing your temper, take a break. Sit still. Breathe. If you are dealing with a situation that could work itself out, doing nothing is viable option. Your partner could realize the error of their ways and make amends, take out the disputed trash, go for the needed treatment or even initiate couples counseling. Regardless, by deliberately doing nothing you can be quietly claiming your sense of equanimity.

Communicate

*In order to get to a healthier and more productive place, we need to
give up our fear of conflict, turmoil and resistance.*
–John Gottman

Sometimes we must fight for the relationship we want. Saying, "I prefer to choose my battles" is a way of avoiding conflict. An argument may be just what you need to clear the air and work out your differences. Couples who are not arguing are probably not connecting. It is not as important how you get into an argument, but that you are able to resolve it. If you are sincere about wanting to improve your conflicts, learn to identify the *Four Horsemen: criticism, contempt, defensiveness* and *stonewalling.* Replace these with healthier, more productive options. While it seems like work, eventually it becomes second nature, and it is less bruising than fighting.

Leave

I got divorced at Christmas. So I bought an electric train set and
nailed it to the dining room table - because I could.
–John Prine

If your relationship is la0cking more of the essentials than it is providing, it's time to reconsider. You can do couples counseling. You can take a time out - a *loving separation.* You can stay physically but check out emotionally. Minimize your time together. House-sit, travel, get an RV, work opposite shifts, move to the basement. It is less disruptive, but feeling lonely while in a relationship might be more painful than going solo. Then there are *toxic situations* such as *domestic violence* in which your strength *is* in the leaving. What is your self respect worth? Learn how to manage *grief, loss and transition.* Learn to love living alone. Leaving a relationship is never easy but reinventing yourself is exciting. Do something to declare your independence. Go to Paris. Get a tattoo. Learn something new. Keep colorful flowers, fresh fruit or lit candies on your table. Decorate with something ridiculous or outrageous - because now, you can.

Solutions Relationship Checklist

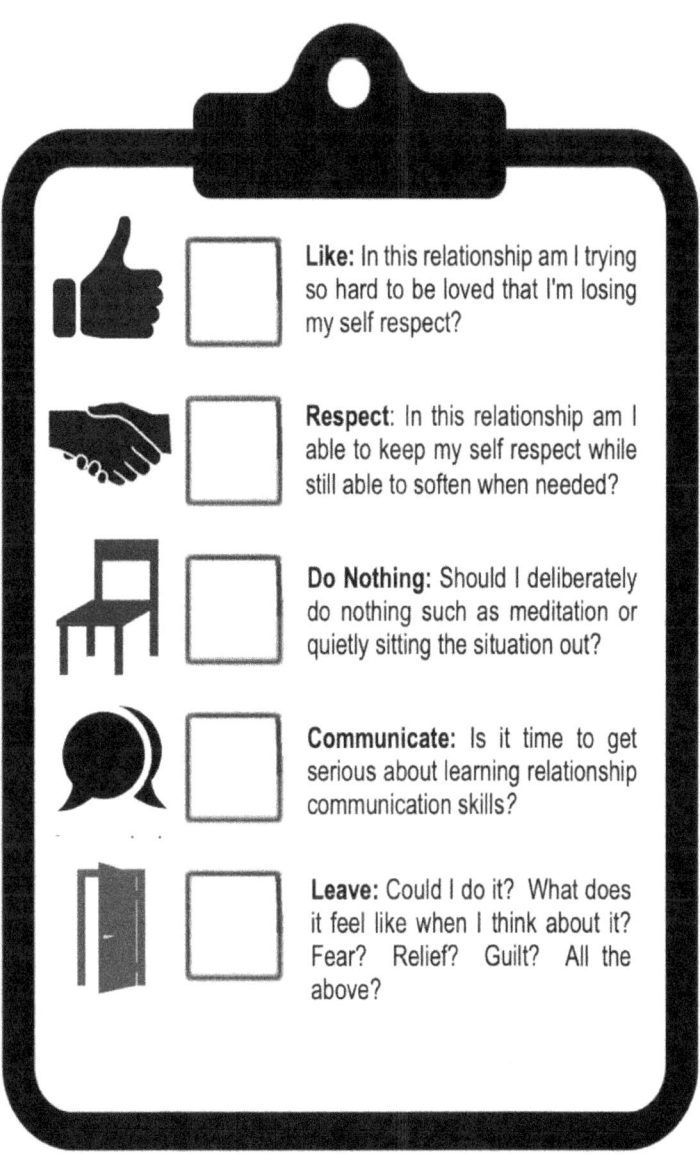

Like: In this relationship am I trying so hard to be loved that I'm losing my self respect?

Respect: In this relationship am I able to keep my self respect while still able to soften when needed?

Do Nothing: Should I deliberately do nothing such as meditation or quietly sitting the situation out?

Communicate: Is it time to get serious about learning relationship communication skills?

Leave: Could I do it? What does it feel like when I think about it? Fear? Relief? Guilt? All the above?

Connected Conversations in Romantic Relationships

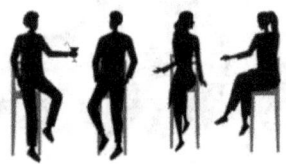

The key to really connecting with someone is identifying what kind of conversation they're trying to have, whether it's a stranger or your spouse of 20 years.

−Charles Duhigg

It seems that often couples who end their relationship are suffering from "irreconcilable communications". It makes me wonder how much emotional intimacy was present when initially dating. A recent search for "relationship meet ups" or "speed dating" indicated many events were being held online or even while working out. Seriously, is this the best way to find an intimate partner? I suggest organizers start in-person events called "Wine, Cheese and Connected Conversations". Within a prescribed time format, assign deeper conversation topics that challenge a person's ability to be authentic and even vulnerable. At the same time, it would be an opportunity to determine the other person's willingness to hold emotional space and really listen. It might even attract more sincere, serious, relationship seekers. If two people can rise to this challenge and share a genuine moment of connection in this environment, there might be hope for their future.

Happily ever after simply means that both partners are known, valued, accepted for who they are and who they are becoming. The goal is to be able to love your partner more deeply each and every year you're together.
— John M. Gottman

CHAPTER 9

Quicksand

When exploring, read the warning signs:

figuratively and literally.

–Mitta Xinindlu

Quicksand

Be careful...not all are what they seem, some people pretend to be the beach but they're actually quicksand.

−Steve Maraboli

We get stuck. We go round and round in a difficult, dysfunctional relationship unable to break free and we ask ourselves how did I get here? In this section we will learn to identify those situations that keep us stuck. Some might be identified as toxic, but keep in mind toxic is not the same for everyone. Kryptonite, peanuts or gluten anyone? While there are a few clearly toxic situations such as *domestic violence* or *sex abuse*, I hesitate to overuse the word. Also, I suggest caution when casually labeling someone with a *personality disorder.* Their behavior may be more a learned way of being in the world. For example, using "narcissistic" to describe what is annoyingly self-centered. One you can live with, the other you probably should not. Same for flag colors. What is a red flag for one person may be yellow, or even green for another.

Intermittent Reinforcement

Reinforcement learning is the idea of being able to assign credit or blame to all the actions you took along the way while you were getting that reward signal.
−Jeff Dean

Experiments in learning found if they consistently rewarded a rat with a pellet every time they pressed a lever, they had a contented rat. If the rat never got a pellet, the rat moved on. However, if they gave only an occasional pellet at random, the rat would stay - obsessively pressing the lever in the hope of an eventual reward. It is the same premise used in gambling, newsfeeds and social media. Our devices are like pellet dispensers, generating a sense of anticipation, excitement and desire. Anyone in our lives can act as a dispenser – employers, friends, family, and partners, intermittently dispensing whatever it is we desire - love, connection, belonging, admiration, security. It is unhealthy and it can keep us stuck.

Adaptation

People only accept change when they are faced with necessity,
and only recognize necessity when a crisis is upon them.
−Jean Monnet

There is an adage that if a frog is put in a pot of boiling water he will jump out. However, if placed in very gradually heating water, he won't notice the heat increasing and will eventually perish. While the logistics of the theory have been debunked, the frog in boiling water has come to mean slowly adapting to any gradually deteriorating situation. Like the frog, it is often easier to stay than it is to jump out when you first notice the problem. Co-dependency can be part of this dynamic. You accommodate, adapt and adjust. You keep trying harder to make things better and might not notice just how bad it has become until it is too late.

Learned Helplessness

Learned helplessness is the giving-up reaction, the quitting response that follows from the belief that whatever you do doesn't matter.
—Arnold Schwarzenegger

The experiment for learned helplessness involved dogs who received a mild shock when attempting to change their circumstances. Eventually those poor pups gave up even after the shock mechanism was turned off. When faced with an ongoing or repeated difficult situation we might make a few attempts at change. For example, we might try to leave our abusive partner only to return when pressured. This can also cause us to form a *trauma bond with* the abuser. Simply giving up can occur in less dramatic situations such as attempting to improve a negative situation at work only to find our concerns fall on deaf ears. When our initial attempts at improving our situation are initially thwarted, even though we can still make it better, we stop trying.

Denial

I'm not in denial, I'm just selective about the reality I accept.

—Bill Watterson

Denial is a type of *defense mechanism or coping strategy* described as sticking your head in the sand or ignoring the elephant in the living room. The *Emperor's New Clothes* is a story to explain *collective denial*. Denial can keep us stuck, ignoring the reality of a situation because the consequences of facing that reality can be devastating. For example, we deny knowledge of our partner's *infidelity* because accepting reality means a difficult confrontation and a possible breakup. We deny *sex abuse* in a family because the only way out is to expose the collusion in the family system. We deny *addiction* and become *co-dependent* ourselves because addiction is such an insidious and seemingly intractable situation. Collectively we deny reality to avoid political or social consequences and we do not want to be the only one to call out the naked emperor.

Gaslighting

Do not adjust your mind - the fault is in reality.

—R.D. Laing

The term "gaslighting" comes from a 1940's movie where the *sociopath* husband makes his wife think she is crazy by randomly adjusting the lighting, hiding things and deliberately making her question her reality. Gaslighting is *not* the same as lying. It's an insidious form of manipulation and control that is often used by *narcissists*, *sociopaths* and *addicts* or *substance abusers.* Victims are systematically and deliberately fed false information that leads them to question what they know to be true, even about themselves. Down becomes up and up becomes down. Ultimately, they end up questioning their memory, their reality, and even their sanity. When you start to think you are crazy, look for gaslighting.

Love Bombing

Abusers are notorious for rushing the first stage of intimacy,
something that's often described by survivors as a kind of
'love-bombing.
—Jess Hill

Love bombing is just what it sounds like. An explosion of expensive gifts and meals, grand gestures, effusive displays of affection, expressions of admiration or unsolicited sexting. (It is called "junk mail" for a reason). You are their soulmate, the center of their world. Initially, it may feel flattering, especially in a new relationship. Beware, it is a *grooming tactic* used by *sexual predators.* Love bombing is also used by *domestic violence* perpetrators in the *cycle of abuse.* One study suggests the behavior is most common in people with *narcissistic* tendencies. It can also be an indicator of an *insecure attachment* style or a *borderline personality disorder.* If you are feeling insecure or struggling with a low *sense of self* or loneliness, you might be vulnerable to love bombing.

Boundaries

Boundaries empower us to determine how we'll be treated

by others.

−Anne Katherine

Boundaries set limits with others, keep you from feeling taken advantage of, and establish the rules of respect. Open borders on boundaries are an invitation for those who tend to push the limits to shove their way in. Set clear boundaries on your time by saying: "I can meet for a quick lunch." If they push: firmly repeat what you just said. Set boundaries on your space. When a date pushes to come inside, you say: "Nope, not tonight." If they push, firmly repeat. Set boundaries on what you do. "I cannot help you this weekend, I have other plans." If they push, firmly repeat. You get the picture. This is not meant to disregard the normal social negations that are part of reciprocity. We also want to be careful that we are not so rigid that no one can get in. Use boundaries to firmly keep a potential violator in check.

Substance Use

It's not the substance that hooks you, it's the emotions...There is a crack somewhere in our spirits, and we have to heal that before anything.
—*Antonio Michael Downing*

If things feel crazy and you can not put your finger on it, look for *addiction*. I describe it as something someone will do to relieve their craving, such as go out in the middle of the night in a snowstorm wearing fuzzy slippers to obtain. This includes alcohol, drugs, smokes, sex, gambling, food, porn or pot. Serious substance abuse is often the underlying cause for many relationship issues as well as toxic behaviors. Until addressed, we will remain stuck. Substance abuse issues are difficult to extricate from. A person with addiction will get help when they are ready, and if they are not ready, they will not. If you are in a relationship with a substance abuser, your job is to take care of yourself. Find an Al Anon or Narcotics Anonymous or other support group. Understand the concepts of *enabling* and *co-dependency*. Your options for any solution are still the three basics: *do nothing, communicate, or leave.*

Stress and Trauma

The paradox of trauma is that it has both the power to destroy and

the power to transform and resurrect.

−Peter A Levine

When any kind of existential threat occurs, our bodies receive a jolt of adrenalin, and we go into *trauma response mode. (Fight, flight, freeze, faint, fawn.)* We are physically, emotionally, and intellectually overwhelmed and everyone processes differently. For example, I was initially puzzled by a client's reaction to a sex assault until she pointed out the relatively recently coined "fawn" response which is more aligned with attempting to please and/ or appease. (I love learning from my clients and students.) Since these are essentially *defense mechanisms,* we may resort to one or more of these responses when faced with ordinary stressful confrontations. These could include our partners, friends, service workers, supervisors, parents, and/or children. Knowing a bit about how your *primitive brain* works under stress may help you mitigate unhelpful response patterns.

Fear of Failure or Fear of Success?

The only person unhappier than a writer whose expectations aren't

fulfilled is one whose dreams come true.

–Stephen King

Fear of failure and fear of success look very similar and seem to be equally paralyzing, Fear of failure keeps us from starting, fear of success keeps us from finishing. For example, encouraging someone to try a community college class or an upgrade in job aspirations. Lack of confidence and fear of failure might keep them mired. On the other hand, I would see good students sabotage their own efforts at the end of the semester and deliberately fail or drop. One student expressed their concern by saying: "If I were to succeed, how would my life change and who would I leave behind?"

Illusion verses Reality

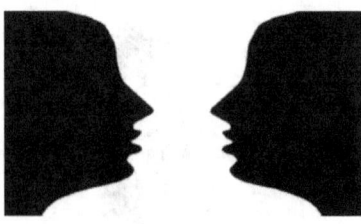

Closure happens right after you accept that letting go is more important than projecting a fantasy of how the relationship could have been.

— *Sylvester McNutt*

It is far more difficult to let go of the illusion than the reality. We hold fast to the fantasy of what could be and deny the reality of our situation. Sometimes we get caught up in the romantic ideal – the hope of "happily ever after". We just cannot let that go. Promises of change keep us hooked: "He promised he'd go to AA." "She swears she will stop seeing him." "He was so sorry he hit me, he promised to go to anger management." "Sorry, no salary increases again, let's talk next year." We have hope, so we let bad behavior go, again. Some choose to remain in an unhealthy relationship dynamic for fear of being alone, lack of resources or not wanting to hurt the feelings of the other person. Take off the rose-colored glasses. Go back to the baseball rule: Three strikes and out.

Anxiety

Our anxiety does not come from thinking about the future, but

from wanting to control it.

— Kahlil Gibran

Anxiety tends to be about the future. It is the "what ifs". "What if I make a fool of myself?" "What if something goes wrong?" "What if I am alone for the rest of my life?" "What if we have an accident.?" The hard truth is many of our "what if" scenarios *are* real possibilities. S**t happens. As a consummate worrier, I assure you, no amount of hand wringing can influence the outcome. What we *can* do is hope for the best, plan, or prep for the worst. Ask: "What is the worst that can happen?" You might be embarrassed, become a social outcast, or yes, you could die. Anxiety could also be a fear of failure or even *fear of success.* Learn to self soothe, take long slow deep breaths. Recite the *Serenity Prayer.* Unless it is life threatening or debilitating, use meditation in lieu of medication.

Depression

*There are wounds that never show on the body that are deeper
and more hurtful than anything that bleeds.*
— Laurell K. Hamilton

My views on depression and the use of anti-depressants may
be controversial. One way I view depression is as "a cocoon of
change", also known as *grief* - normal and necessary for transition and loss. Another view is depression as "anger turned in-
ward". This is the passive individual coping with cumulative pain
and hurt from toxic relationship(s). A third view is depression as
an "outcome of loneliness and isolation". This is exacerbated
by social media and our post pandemic preference for remote
work. In my experience, these can be worked through by talk
therapy and/or life changes, without medication. A fourth view of
depression is "organic and biochemical". This is that dark intractable clinical depression which *is* best managed by medication,
therapy, group support and life changes. Before committing to
pharmaceuticals, give serious thought to which kind of depression you may be struggling with.

Ennui

I am tired of myself tonight. I should like to be somebody else.
— *Oscar Wilde*

I love the word *ennui*. Pronounced "on whee" and when said, I visualize a 1920's drama queen putting the back of her hand to her forehead saying: "Alas, I have ennui". It is a French word that essentially means being bored, or "world weary", especially from a life of too much ease (or maybe too much cannabis?) Although it looks and feels somewhat similar to depression, it is not an official medical diagnosis and anti-depressants are probably not going to be helpful. Treatment, at the risk of sounding too direct, consists of "getting a life". Get off the couch and away from your device or TV. Engage with the outside world, change things up, move your body, get out in nature, try on anything that interest you. Travel, volunteer. Find meaning and purpose.

You don't ever have to feel guilty about
removing toxic people from your life. It
doesn't matter whether someone is a relative,
romantic interest, employer, childhood friend
or a new acquaintance - you don't have to
make room for people who cause you pain
or make you feel small. . . if a person disregards
your feelings, ignores your boundaries,
and continues to treat you in a harmful way,
they need to go. –Daniell Koepke

CHAPTER 10

Transitions

*It's not so much that we're afraid of change or so in
love with the old ways, but it's that place in between
that we fear . . .It's like being between trapezes.
It's Linus when his blanket is in the dryer. There's
nothing to hold on to.*

— Marilyn Ferguson

Transition and Loss

For we lose not only by death, but also by leaving and being left, by changing and letting go and moving on.

−Judith Viorst

Life and relationships mean transitions - even the good ones in-volve loss. We get a promotion and miss our colleagues. We get married and miss time with friends. We have a baby and miss sleep. We finish a project and miss the creative energy. Then there are difficult life transitions such as losing a job, getting divorced, moving away or launching our last child. Eventually we all confront illness and death. Some will experience natu-ral disasters and the loss of their home. War and mass shoot-ings cause incomprehensible loss and devastation. Often this means the death of someone's son or daughter. Unlike orphan or widow[er}, did you know there is no word in our vocabulary to describe someone who has lost their child? Bottom line: transi-tion and loss are inevitable, unique and relative.

Stages

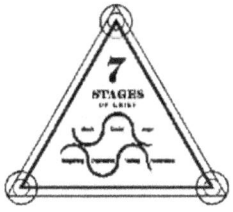

Any natural, normal human being, when faced with any kind of loss,

will go from shock all the way through acceptance.

–Elisabeth Kübler-Ross

Knowing what to expect when dealing with transition and loss may alleviate some discomfort. The basic stages are *shock, denial, anger, bargaining, depression, testing/exploring and, acceptance.* Not necessarily in that order. For example, consider discovering your favorite restaurant unexpectedly closed. *Shock*: "Whaaaaat?" *Denial*: This is *not* happening." *Anger*: "Damn it, what's up with these people?" *Bargaining*: "Check the door, maybe they forgot to change the sign." *Depression*: "I am so bummed." *Testing/Exploring*: "Let's check out the new place down the block." *Acceptance*: "This is great." This simple situation shows how we can pass through all the stages for a minor incident in less than a minute. Major transitions and losses can take years and the process is not always linear.

Shock

The loneliest moment in someone's life is when they are watching

their whole world fall apart, and all they can do is stare blankly.

—*F. Scott Fitzgerald*

Suppose you just discovered your life-long best friend and business partner has cleared out the all the company assets and fled the country with your intimate partner. Your home was used as collateral for the business and the lease is up on your car. This is a very bad moment for you. Transition and change are difficult enough when planned. When it is suddenly thrust upon you, some level of shock is likely. Whatever reaction you have right now is "normal" and could run the gamut of flight, fight, faint, fawn or freeze. You might start doing crazy things like throwing her stuff out the window or lay naked on the front lawn kicking and screaming. Or you might just sit and stare at the wall for a very long time. To an outsider, it might seem you have lost your mind, however, since we each process events differently, expect the unexpected.

Denial

Denial helps us to pace our feelings of grief. There is a grace in denial. It is nature's way of letting in only as much as we can handle.

–Elisabeth Kubler-Ross and David Kessler

Denial is often the first response to a loss such as a breakup, death of a loved one, serious diagnosis or loss of a job. It is a common defense mechanism that protects us from the pain and shock of bad news. "The doctor must have made a mistake." "Mother is not dead; she's only just sleeping." "The boss was just having a bad day and will soon realize how essential I am." "They'll come back; they can't live without me." A widow or widower may continue to have discussions with the deceased (not uncommon with people who live alone). We might become numb and check out of social interactions. If this, or any stage continues acutely for more than a year, it could be diagnosed as complicated grief or *bereavement disorder* and professional help, or a support group is recommended.

Anger

Resentment is like drinking poison and then hoping it will
kill your enemies.
−Nelson Mandela

For many, feeling angry is easier than feeling sad. Anger feels more powerful and is a way to avoid feeling pain. You would expect to feel angry toward the partner who just threw you and your belongings to the curb. It would be normal to rage against the employer who just escorted you out with the cardboard box of shame. If you are not prone to anger, this reaction may surprise you - especially when directed to a loved one who just died. Then we add guilt to the mix. This is the stage we ask the "Why me?" questions. Anger may overflow to others. If you are struggling with a contentious breakup, avoid letting your anger bleed over to your children − it poisons their already fragile souls. If we are still stuck in resentment and bitterness beyond a year or so, it is likely a result of avoiding the painful stage of grief. I have heard spouses still dissing each other fifty years after a contentious divorce. Seriously?

Bargaining

We will do anything not to feel the pain of this loss. We remain in the past, trying to negotiate our way out of the hurt.

—David Kessler

This is the "If only." stage. It is an internal and external negotiation. If it is a breakup, this is where we grovel and make ridiculous promises of change. If a pending job loss, we offer suggestions for our own improvement. If an illness, we say we will change unhealthy behaviors or try a new miracle cure. For the death of a loved one, we ask what we could have done to prevent it from happening. We develop a relationship with God and start asking for divine intervention. This is where the aphorism "There are no atheists in foxholes or on turbulent airplanes" originates. Essentially you say you are willing to do anything to make this awfulness go away. It is an accompaniment to hope and a necessary stage to attempt to gain control of a downwardly spiraling situation.

Grief

Grief is a normal and natural response to loss. Keeping grief inside increases your pain.

—Anne Grant

Do not skip this stage! People try to avoid it, often with anti-depressants or substances. It stems from the fear that the tears will never stop. They will stop, and you *can* stop them. Realize grief comes in rogue waves so be prepared. Keep tissues handy. When an unexpected wave comes in public, find a restroom or go to your car and let it go. Plan solo, sober, grieving time. Hang out a "do not disturb" sign. Wrap yourself in a cozy blanket. Listen to sad music. Peruse old photos and mementos. Journal, eat comfort food. Wallow, weep and sleep. If you skip this stage, the cumulative grief will show up later and you might find yourself having a meltdown over the death of a goldfish. Closure begins when you are ready to put those treasured mementos away and move toward exploring new ways of being in the world.

Exploring

Ruins, for me, are the beginning. With the debris you can construct
new ideas. They are symbols of a beginning.
−Anselm Kiefer

This is the "dressing room" phase. Exploring new ideas, new ways of living in this new reality. It means stretching your emotional muscles, taking small risks. If it is the loss of a job, time to polish up your self respect and go on the search sites or give serious thought to a new endeavor. If it is a loss of relationship, through break up or death, it might be time to get out there and socialize. If you meet someone interesting, go slow, this is not the time for any sudden moves. It is a good time to try new things. Join a travel club. Explore new places. Consider relocating to a community better suited to your new situation. Ask yourself what you enjoyed doing in your life prior to your relationship or current career. Maybe its time to dust off that fishing rod, buy that cute convertible or take up Salsa dancing.

Acceptance

Healing doesn't mean the loss didn't happen. It means that it no longer controls us.
—David Kessler

Some people feel guilty about being happy and/or moving on. Acceptance is not letting go of your love for the person or even being at peace with what happened. It is finding closure and a way to live your life going forward. You might even have reached acceptance only to find yourself angry or sad all over again. If so, go back to the grieving stage, you still have some work to do. Reaching acceptance does not mean the pain of a deep loss goes away, but finding meaning and purpose in the loss can help. This is why we see the parents of children killed in mass shootings campaigning for gun control. It is a way for them to restore their sense of equilibrium. Acceptance does not necessarily mean the pain, or the memory goes away, we just find a place inside ourselves that makes it more comfortable.

We resist transition not because we can't
accept the change, but because we can't
accept letting go of that piece of ourselves
that we have to give up when and
because the situation has changed.

–William Bridges

CHAPTER 11

Living Well

For everyone, well-being is a journey. The secret is committing to that journey and taking those first steps with hope and belief in yourself.

–Deepak Chopra

Living Well

The good life is a process, not a state of being. It is a direction,

not a destination.

−Carl Rogers

My personal mantra is "Living well is knowing who you are, what you feel, what you want, and how you are going to get there." After getting my advanced degree, my plan was to eventually start a private practice. I was also ready for a healthy relationship, so I set my intent to find a "sensitive new age, well educated, outdoor traveling companion who shares my love for acoustic music." Soon, I was introduced to my partner by a mutual friend and also had a placement working toward licensure. Thirty plus years later, now semi-retired, my life partner and I are still playing music and exploring the outdoors. While not without struggles, it has been a great life. It never would have happened had I not taken the steps to learn who I am, what I am feeling, what I want and how to get there.

Who Am I?

How lovely to know you don't have to be perfect, all you need to do is just be.

–Jeffrey Marsh

Developing an *authentic sense of self* is essential for successful relationships. Embrace self-discovery. Find a therapist or life coach that is a good fit. Start or attend a Simplifying Relationship Seminar (see Chapter 13). Take the free online Big 5 Personality Test. Circle adjectives to describe yourself from the list in the appendix. Read self-help books, listen to podcasts. Search for topics of interest from accessible, credible sources such as *Psychology Today* magazine. Find and post inspirations. Identify and embrace your positive personality characteristics as well as your "shadow side". It is both that make us human. Practice self acceptance. We are who we are because of characteristics we are born with and those we develop because of our environment - the "nature verses nurture" debate. You cannot change something until you quit fighting it. Then it's power often dissipates, and you learn to live with it.

Your Big Five

Write down your results from
the Big Five Personality Test.
Look up more about each ome
and how it impacts you and your life.

_____

_____

_____

_____

_____

What Am I Feeling?

Our emotions tell us what to value. They're like a little GPS system.
Go that way. Don't go that way.
—David Brooks

We can not know what we want unless we know how we feel. Yes, the dreaded "F" word. Due to long embedded social anxiety and fear of subsequent rejection, acknowledgement and expression of emotion is awkward and difficult for most people. Fortunately, it is now being taught in elementary school and the animated film *Inside Out* introduced us to the emotions *anger, depression, joy, fear, disgust, embarrassment, envy and ennui.* To help clients determine what they want, I look for the light (or darkness) in their eyes when they express themselves. However, since many of our emotions are initially uncomfortable, some choose to mitigate this with anti-depressants or anti-anxiety medications. I realize at times they may be necessary, but they tend to subtly dim our internal signals. It is like driving at night with dirty headlights. We get where we are going but miss much along the way.

Feeling Words Exercise

Look for *feeling words*. Set a timer and every few hours. write down what word best describes what you are feeling at that exact moment. Keep it up until it becomes second nature.

_____

_____

_____

_____

_____

_____

_____

_____

_____

What Do I Want?

Whatever your dreams are, start taking them very, very seriously.

−Barbara Sher

All too often we end up doing not what we really want to be doing but what others have in mind for us. It is called *identity foreclosure*. It is living life in a blur of the voices of others and their expectations. Eventually we lose ourselves. We stop dreaming. So now, (re)discover what is important to you. This is like the dressing room. You try on your ideas and interests. Toss out those that do not fit. Be curious about *you*. Start by noticing those small moments that give you joy. Pay attention to what or who draws you in no matter how insignificant. Make a note of what you like to read. Spend time alone in nature. Travel solo. What do you do when you have time to yourself? What makes your eyes sparkle? What gave you joy as a child? Who were you before you became an adult?

What Do I Really Want?

Find a quiet moment. Ask yourself over and over:" What do I really want?" Jot it down. Do not edit. It can be silly or serious, real or impossible. A sentence or a word.
Just do it - again and again.

_____

_____

_____

_____

_____

_____

_____

_____

_____

_____

How You are Going to Get there

Of any stopping place in life, it is good to ask whether it will be a good place from which to go on as well as a good place to remain.
−Mary Catherine Bateson

Imagine your life as a patchwork quilt with mixed up pieces sewn together. Much of what you have already experienced is leading you to where you want to go. You may even discover you are already living your best life, you just needed to be reminded of it. You do not need to decide right now on a specific goal or course of action until the time is right to consider a change. However, if you do have a specific goal or dream in mind, commit to what you want. Imagine what it is going to look like. Research how it is done. Formulate a plan. Let others know your intentions and ask for help. Allow yourself occasional moments of doubt but keep moving forward. Once you start, getting there often presents itself and now it is time to enjoy the ride.

Moving Forward

Ask: "What do I need to do to move forward with my dreams or plans?" Make it doable such as: "Research cost of X." or "Ask so and so about Y." "Look up how to..." Keep it simple. Keep adding ideas.

_____

_____

_____

_____

_____

_____

_____

_____

_____

You have brains in your head. You have feet in your shoes. You can steer yourself in any direction you choose. You're on your own, and you know what you know. And you are the guy who'll decide where to go.

–Dr. Suess

CHAPTER 12

Flourishing

Happiness is not out there for us to find.

The reason that it's not out there is that it's

inside us.

—Sonja Lyubomirsky

Flourishing

Don't ask yourself what the world needs. Ask yourself what makes
you come alive. And then go and do that. Because what the world
needs is people who have come alive.
−Tal Ben Shahar

You have learned how to live your best life, and now you are
ready to flourish! In the late 1990's psychologist Martin Seligman
turned the psychological world upside down by suggesting we
focus on happiness and thriving, instead of mental illness. He
asked the question: If we can measure depression, why can't we
measure happiness? He and his research teams then set about
defining not only what makes people happy, but what makes
them thrive and flourish. This does not mean being annoyingly happy all the time, known as *toxic positivity.* It means living
our best life, focusing on fulfillment, contentment, satisfaction
and well being. To that end, this *positive psychology* movement
narrowed down five elements to flourishing: *Positive Emotion,*
Engagement and Flow, Healthy Relationships, Meaning and
Purpose, Achievement. (PERMA).

Happy Nuns

*Beautiful young people are accidents of nature, but beautiful old
people are works of art.*

−Eleanor Roosevelt

In one positive psychology study, researchers examined the relationship between positive emotions and longevity in a lengthy
study of 180 nuns. Chosen because health issues and lifestyle
were similar - diet, and bad "habits" such as smoking or drinking
were almost nil. They examined the autobiographical sketches
they wrote as part of their religious vows - written when the sis-
ters were about 22 years old and just beginning their careers
with the church. They discovered that the nuns who expressed
more positive emotions in their initial writings or continued to
write optimistically about experiences in their lives, lived on
average 10 years longer than those whose writing reflected a
more negative or dour point of view.

We Are in Control

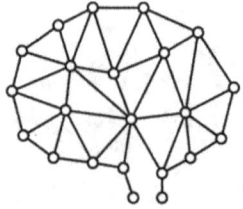

Your brain is the organ of your personality, character, and intelligence and is heavily involved in making you who you are.

—Daniel G. Amen

The study of positive psychology revealed that we have far more control of our happiness than we initially realized. Fifty percent of our happiness is essentially our genetic "set point"- our general disposition - what we are born with. Are you more like Eeyore or more like Tigger? Only 10% of happiness is life, work and circumstances - so as much as you hope that new car, partner, job or house will make a difference - not so much. In fact, this is called the *hedonic treadmill* - we quickly return to a relatively stable level of happiness despite major positive or negative events or life changes. We can, however, improve our overall well-being by a whopping 40% by consciously changing how our brain is wired by adapting the techniques to follow.

Positive Emotion

When we take time to notice the things that go right - it means
we're getting a lot of little rewards throughout the day.
−Martin Seligman

We can change the wiring in our brains to offset negative with positive emotion through a daily practice of *reframing, savoring* and *gratitude. Reframing* is spin doctoring annoying circumstances. Lose a sock in the dryer? - "Maybe it just needs some alone time." Stuck in traffic? - "A good time to call grandma." *Savoring* is using your five senses to notice what delights you. *Feel* the cool side of the pillow. *Smell* the spring lilacs. *See* the great view. *Hear* the silence. *Taste* the spice. *Gratitude* is acknowledging the little things. Finding socks that *do* match. The rain stopped. Or consider this example from a precocious child in a school Thanksgiving presentation: "I'm grateful to Little Caesar's because they have breadsticks." A daily practice of these small exercises eventually becomes second nature. Ultimately you will start to notice an improvement in how you view life.

Engagement and Flow

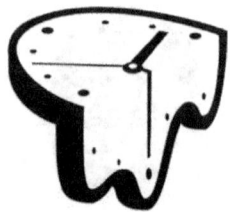

Enjoyment appears at the boundary between boredom and anxiety,
when the challenges are just balanced with the person's capacity
to act.
— *Mihaly Csikszentmihalyi*

Engagement and flow are when you are so involved in whatever you are doing that you completely lose track of time. Sometimes called "being in the zone". It can happen while skiing fresh powder, knitting a scarf, painting a masterpiece, cleaning the garage, prepping a meal, organizing the soup cans or even analyzing data. The idea is you are *doing or creating* something as opposed to being passively entertained. For engagement and flow to be ideal, it should take place in that "sweet spot" between being too easy and too difficult. If too easy, we get bored and distracted. If too difficult we get frustrated and quit. If you do not have something that gives you that sense of flow, try doing something new. If you are not sure, note those times when you are experiencing engagement and flow and do it more often.

Relationships

Man is by nature a social animal.

–Aristotle

In these disconnected times, it is worth being reminded that much of our happiness and well-being is based on healthy, in-person relationships with others. As an exercise, set aside three times a week for a focused in-person interaction with someone else. This can be coffee, lunch, a walk, a game night, a concert. Go to what sociologists call a *third space*, separate from home and work or school. Think of it as a "hang out" place that "regulars" go. Become a "regular" yourself. This can be a coffee shop, a cafe, a bar, a church, a community center, a library, a makerspace, a park, a theatre, a bookstore, a concert hall, a sport venue. Organize a "connected conversations" gathering or a Simplifying Relationships Seminar. A sense of belonging serves to reduce our progressively destructive sense of isolation, increases our *social capital,* improves our overall well-being and is catching!

Meaning and Purpose

Deprived of meaningful work, men and women lose their reason for existence; they go stark, raving mad.

−Fyodor Dostoevsky

Viktor Frankl's influential book *Man's Search for Meaning*, was written while a prisoner in a Nazi concentration camp. Frankl noted that those who fared the best in those horrific circumstances were able to find meaning by completing small tasks, caring for others or facing their suffering with dignity. The positive psychology research teams found similar results when evaluating the life history and examining the brains of individuals who had led long, healthy and productive lives. We all need a sense of meaning and purpose. It does not matter if it is grandiose or small. If your contribution is to make coffee for your AA meeting or book club, that is meaning and purpose. It can be what you do for your work, how you care for your family, or how you show up for friends and community. Ask yourself: "What did I do today that helped someone else and gave meaning and purpose to my life?"

Achievement

My success lies in having achieved a record number of failures.
−Ashleigh Brilliant

A sense of achievement, no matter how small, can greatly improve our well being. While it might be grand to win an Olympic
gold medal, every four years is just not often enough. We need
a sense of accomplishment daily. This can be something as
simple as cleaning the fridge, getting a load of laundry done
or finishing a tough homework assignment. (I am just thrilled
when Wordle rewards me with the occasional "impressive!")
While *extrinsic rewards* such as gold stars and trophies - how
about "Most Improved Camper"? are commonplace in elementary school, we do not tend to acknowledge our accomplish-
ments as we get older. Daily, reward yourself with a metaphor-
ical gold star or trophy for those small achievements or steps
taken toward a larger goal. That *intrinsic reward* and feeling of
satisfaction for a "job well done" adds one more element to your
increasingly flourishing life.

Character Strengths

If Positive Psychology teaches us anything, it is that all of us are

a mixture of strengths and weaknesses. No one has it all

and no one lacks it all.

−Christopher Peterson

By taking the online VIA Character Strengths Assessment, I learned to operate from my top strengths of Humor, Creativity, Honesty, Appreciation of Excellence and Beauty and Social Intelligence. It was freeing and life changing. (I also came to appreciate having a partner whose top strengths countered my weaknesses.) I started letting clients know in advance that I have a wicked sense of humor, I would be direct and honest in giving feedback and may offer quirky, creative ideas and suggestions. I also warn them I am likely to curse since, according to the VIA, I have no sense of Self-Regulation or Prudence. Using my strengths re-energized my practice and gave me confidence to be my authentic self. Spend a few minutes, take the online VIA Survey, and learn more about operating from *your* strengths and find ways to compensate for those areas that are not your strong suit.

Character Strengths Exercise

List your top ten-character strengths
here. Can be used as a personal
growth seminar discussion topic.

_____

_____

_____

_____

_____

_____

_____

_____

_____

_____

Flourishing goes beyond happiness or
satisfaction with life. True, people who
flourish are happy. But that's not the half of it.
Beyond feeling good, they're also doing
good-adding value to the world.
–Barbara Fredrickson

CHAPTER 13

Groups and Seminars

Members of a cohesive group feel warmth and comfort

in the group and a sense of belongingness; they value

the group and feel in turn that they are valued,

accepted, and supported by other members.

—Irvin D. Yalom

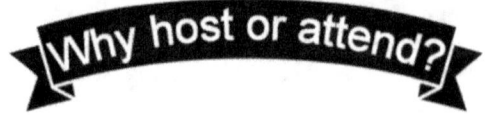
Why host or attend?

Organizing a Simplifying Relationship group or seminar gives attendees the invaluable opportunity to share experiences and get validation from others. It also offers a more economical and in-person, socially connected option for personal growth than individual therapy. For the mental health professional, it is an opportunity to develop or refresh their practice and serve a greater number of people. Since this book touches on issues experienced by most of us sooner or later, following the chapters in order gives a sense of predictability. It works for weekly or monthly meetings or a multi day retreat. While the ideal group is facilitated by a mental health professional, life coach, or teacher, I realize that may not always be possible and a peer led group is a viable option. This chapter will offer some basic guidelines to organizing and facilitating an in person, Simplifying Relationships group or seminar.

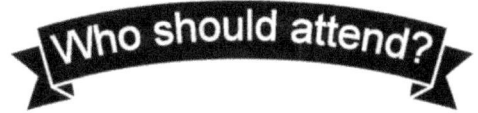

Who should attend?

Decide in advance who you would like to attend. Of course it fits for anyone struggling with to understand their relationships with other people. But you might want to be more specific. Women under 30? Men over 40? How about a high school or college group? LGBTQ focused? Or choose not to specify and appreciate the diversity of attendees. Reach out via social media, meetup and or posters at work or school. A manageable number for an interactive seminar is between about five and ten people. Once you have all the sign ups you are looking for, the group should be closed after the first meeting. Trust and vulnerability take time to develop so people coming and going is not recommended. In addition, this is best run as a "softly structured" format based on consecutive book chapters that build on one another and shared experiences.

Where to host.

It is essential that your choice of location be accessible, comfortable, quiet and private. Seating should be open and circular with no large table in between. (Think support group style model). Back room of a coffee shop, a church, a community center room, private space at the library, your resident clubhouse, or a small hotel conference room will work. The space needs to be available on all the dates you have chosen. If you are comfortable and know something about your attendees, a private home is also an option. Keep tissues handy and encourage attendees to bring own water bottle. If you plan to include refreshments such as coffee, tea, or cookies as an icebreaker, make sure the facility allows for this and of course clean up after.

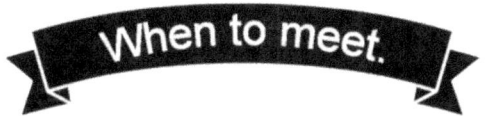

When to meet.

Chose a time when most people can attend without other commitments. A weeknight or a Saturday might be best. If you plan to follow the book chapters, schedule for twelve weeks, 90 minutes each. Some chapters may move more quickly than others or you could end up leaving some unfinished. Remind attendees that doing their own research and homework in between sessions is essential to being able to manage it within the time frame. Plan to arrive a few minutes before and stay a few moments after for social and/or process time. In advance of starting, it would be wise to remind everyone that keeping their contributions to less than ten minutes ensures everyone has the opportunity to process and share their stories or experience. When someone is going over their time, find a silent second to interrupt, thank them and tactfully remind them their time is up.

How to facilitate

The word facilitate means to make something easy and ultimately everyone takes responsibility for the functioning of the group. Ask everyone to review the ethical issues, expectations, and do's. Start by introducing yourself and what brought you here. Then: "who would like to go next?" Sit quietly, someone will break the silence. When most have shared, identify something you found interesting or compelling in the first chapter. Set the tone by communicating from the heart. Ask the group for thoughts or feedback. Process for a few moments, then ask again: "who's next?" Give plenty of time for the reticent to warm up. Use the same format for every meeting. Be flexible, but following the chapters discourages deteriorating into a rambling complaint session. In addition, the chapters are designed to build on one another beginning with less emotionally charged topics, moving through those more difficult and ultimately ending on a positive note.

Ethical Issues

Regardless of the qualifications of the facilitator or the background of the attendees, the same ethical issues apply:

- Confidentiality - what is said in the room stays in the room. Who attends is nobody's business but their own.
- Everyone in attendance shall be considered a "mandatory reporter". If it becomes known that a child's physical well being is in jeopardy protective services is to be notified.
- Everyone has a "duty to warn" in the event of a clear and imminent threat to another person or persons or clear suicidal ideation is presented by a member.
- Since this is a personal growth seminar, rather than a support group, AA or therapy group, the decision to socialize outside the group should be decided by the participants themselves.

What to expect

Knowing what to expect in advance helps keep from being surprised or knocked off center. Tuckman's stage model of group development, commonly known as "forming, storming, norming, performing and adjourning" will most likely manifest itself in some form. Participants will initially be somewhat reserved. Soon some will begin to challenge the facilitator and/or each other, overtly or covertly. (Sit still, breathe, look to others for support, suggest a break.) Ultimately, they will settle in and become contributors and co-facilitators. Eventually, it will be time to process the ending. Expect "triggered meltdowns" - someone becoming tearful and emotional. This is a good thing - it means they felt safe enough in the group to allow repressed grief or trauma to finally break through. Sit still, breathe. Surreptitiously hand them a tissue. but do not attempt to physically comfort or make a big deal - it only serves to distract and/or embarrass them.

Do's

- Read the chapter in advance of the meeting.
- Communicate from the heart. (See appendix.)
- Remember, if you can put "I think" in front, it is from your head.
- Complete the chapter checklists in advance of the meetings.
- Contribute more information on the topics at hand.
- Bring your tools to the second meeting for "show and tell".
- Listen respectfully. hold space and validate the feelings of others.
- Avoid judgement, offering unsolicited solutions or asking "why".
- Do ask:
  - "What is that like for you?"
  - "What do you need most right now?
- Share laughter and humor.
- Enjoy the process.
- Relax!

Appendix

Feeling Words

If you can put "I think" in front of it, it is a thought, not an emotion. i.e.: "I think cold" - it doesn't work.

Anger

Affronted Aggravated Annoyed Antagonistic Belligerent Bitter Burned up Crabby Cranky Enraged Exasperated Fuming Furious Heated Hostile Ill-tempered Incensed Indignant Infuriated Irate Irritated Jealous Offended Outraged Provoked Resentful Seething Sore Spiteful Storming Testy Ticked off Truculent Vengeful Vindictive

Caring

Adoring Admiring Affectionate Appreciative Ardent Attentive Attached Cherishing Compassionate Considerate Crazy about Devoted Doting Fervent Fond Friendly Huggy Idolizing Infatuated Interested in Kind-hearted Like Loving Partial Passionate Respecting Soft on Sympathetic Tender Tolerant Thoughtful Trusting Warm-hearted Warm-toward Wild about Worshipful

Confused

Adrift Ambivalent Baffled Befuddled Bewildered Blurred Chaotic Confounded Confused Disconcerted Disordered Disorganized Distracted Disquieted Disturbed Dizzy Flustered Foggy Frozen Frustrated Misled Mistaken Misunderstood Mixed up Perplexed Puzzled Rattled Reeling Shocked Shook up Speechless Startled Stumped Stunned Taken-aback Thrown Trapped Troubled Uncertain Undecided Unsettled Unsure

Fearful

Afraid Alarmed Anxious Apprehensive Awkward Appalled Careful Cautious Defensive Desperate Distressed Disquieted Fearful Fidgety Fretful Frightened Horrified Intimidated Jumpy Nervous Panicky Paralyzed Petrified Scared Shaky Shy Skittish Shocked Spineless Taut Tense Terrified Terror Timid Threatened Troubled Uneasy Unsure Wrecked Wired Watchful Worried

Happy

Aglow Buoyant Cheerful Contented Cool Delighted Ebullient Ecstatic Elated Energetic Enthusiastic Euphoric Elevated Excited Exhilarated Fine Genial Glad Gleeful Gratified Jovial Keen Light-hearted Lively Merry Overjoyed Pleasant Pleased Riding High Satisfied Serene Sparkling Thrilled Tickled pink Turned on Up Vibrant Zippy Zestful

Hurt

Abused Aching Anguished Annoyed Belittled Cheapened Criticized Crushed Damaged Degraded Destroyed Devalued Discredited Distressed Devastated Discarded Disgraced Forsaken Humiliated I Injured Let down Maligned Marred Miffed Minimized Mistreated Mocked Neglected Punished Put down Rejected Ridiculed Rueful Ruined Resentful Scorned Tender Touched Tortured Troubled Unhappy Used Wounded

inadequate

Ailing Blemished Broken Crippled Damaged Defeated Deficient Dopey Dry Feeble Finished Flawed Helpless Impaired Imperfect Impotent Incapable Incompetent Incomplete Ineffective Inferior Invalid Inept Insignificant Lacking Lame Overwhelmed Meager Powerless Puny Small Substandard Unimportant Tenuous Tiny Uncertain Unconvincing Unsure Useless Washed up Weak Wishful Whipped Worthless Zero

Lonely

Abandoned Alienated Alone Apart Black Blue Cheerless Companionless Cut off Dejected Despondent Deserted Destroyed Detached Empty Estranged Excluded Forsaken Isolated Left out Leftover Lonely Marooned Neglected Oppressed Ostracized Outcast Rejected Shunned Uncherished Detached Discouraged Distant Insulated Melancholy Remote Separate Withdrawn

Sad

Alienated Awful Beaten Bleak Blue Crestfallen Dejected Demoralized Depressed Devalued Desolate Despair Despondent Discouraged Dispirited Distressed Dismal Dispirited Downcast Downhearted Empty Gloomy Glum Grieved Grim Hopeless Lost Low Melancholy Miserable Moody Morose Regretful Rotten Somber Subdued Sorrowful Tearful Unhappy Woeful Worried

Remorse

Abashed Apologetic Ashamed Bashful Blushing Chagrined Chastened Contrite Crestfallen Culpable Debased Degraded Delinquent Demeaned Depraved Disgraced Downhearted Embarrassed Evil Exposed Flustered Guilty Hesitant Humble Humiliated Judged Meek Mortified Penitent Regretful Remorseful Repentant Shamed Shamefaced Sheepish Sorrowful Sorry Sinful Wicked Wrong

Communicate from the Heart

Connections are made with the heart, not the tongue.

−Unknown

Communicating from the heart simply means adding a feeling word describing an emotion to whatever it is you are trying to express. In the seminars it is suggested you find a topic or quote or something that resonates with you to share. Let's take the first quote in Chapter One by Confucius: *Life is really simple, but we insist on making it complicated.* A standard response might be: "I agree with the quote, it makes sense. As a society we do tend to over complicate our world." While this is fine, it does not let me see inside to know a bit more about you - your authentic self. Try this instead, noting the feeling words in bold: "When I read that quote, I felt **grounded**. It helped put me back on my original path. I have a tendency, especially when feeling **anxious**, to complicate things until I'm tripping over my own shoelaces and making a mess. Since one of my personal mantras has always been "KISS" (Keep it Simple Stupid), revisiting this quote really resonated when I needed it most - while trying to finish this book."

I hope you found this book helpful. Use it as a launching place to learn more. Many of those quoted have much more to teach us. Please recommend the book to others and use it to form deeper connections.

 Jody Andrews has over 30 years experience as a Licensed Marriage and Family Therapist, Affiliate Psychology Professor and Seminar Facilitator. www.jodyandrews.com

www.ingramcontent.com/pod-product-compliance
Lightning Source LLC
Chambersburg PA
CBHW070709130626
46553CB00005B/1910